THE PURPLE SHALL GOVERN

A South African A to Z of Nonviolent Action

THE PURPLE SHALL GOVERN

A SOUTH AFRICAN A to Z of NONVIOLENT ACTION

Edited by Dene Smuts and Shauna Westcott

Research by Margaret Nash, Karen Visser, Lou Haysom and Joanne Harvey

1991
OXFORD UNIVERSITY PRESS
CENTRE FOR INTERGROUP STUDIES
CAPE TOWN

Oxford University Press

Walton Street, Oxford OX2 6DP, United Kingdom

OXFORD NEW YORK TORONTO

DELHI BOMBAY CALCUTTA MADRAS KARACHI

PETALINGJAYA SINGAPORE HONG KONG TOKYO

NAIROBI DAR ES SALAAM CAPE TOWN

MELBOURNE AUCKLAND

and associated companies in

BERLIN IBADAN

Centre for Intergroup Studies

Rondebosch, Cape Town

ISBN 0 19 570695 9

Copublished by Oxford University Press Southern Africa, Harrington House, Barrack Street, Cape Town 8001, South Africa, and the Centre for Intergroup Studies, 37 Grotto Road, Rondebosch 7700, South Africa.

Page design and typesetting by Welma Odendaal using Apple Macintosh.

Production assistance by Desktop Technologies.

Printed and bound by Clyson Press, Maitland, Cape.

CONTENTS

ACKNOWLEDGEMENTS

The publication of this book would not have been possible without a generous donation from the Friedrich Ebert Stiftung, to whom the Centre is very grateful for their continuing support.

The original research was based on the categories of nonviolent action as defined in Gene Sharp's classic, *The Methods of Nonviolent Action* (Boston, Horizon Books, 1973), and some quotations from his book have been used to clarify and inform. We gratefully acknowledge him and his work as providing the academic and conceptual framework for *The Purple Shall Govern - A South African A to Z of Nonviolent Action*.

We are grateful to the following publishers and authors for permission to use quotations and extracts from their books:

- David Philip Publisher for "Sanctions, Loans and the South African Economy" by Alan Hirsch in *Sanctions Against Apartheid* edited by Mark Orkin, 1989
- Michael Joseph Ltd for *Move Your Shadow* by Joseph Lelyveld, 1986
- Robson Books Ltd for *The Words of Martin Luther King Jnr* by C Scott King, 1984
- Skotaville Publishers for *The Theory and Practice of Black Resistance to Apartheid* by Mokgethi Notlhabi, 1984, and *Hammering Swords into Ploughshares – Essays in Honour of Archbishop Mpilo Desmond Tutu* edited by Buti Tlhagale and Itumeleng Mosala, 1986
- William Heinemann Ltd for *Mahatma Gandhi, His Life and Influence* by Chandra Kumar and Mohinder Puri, 1982

The extract on page 59 was reprinted with permission of Macmillan Publishing Company from *Freedom Rising* by James North. © Copyright 1985 by James North.

We should also like to acknowledge with thanks:

- Pan Books for *Another day of life* by Rysard Kapuscinski, 1988
- Hoover Institution Press for *From Protest to Challenge* Vol II by T Karis and G Carter, 1987
- Africa World Press Inc for "Lessons from the Sarmcol Strike" by D Bonnin and A Sitas in W Cobbet and R Cohen (eds): *Popular Struggles in South Africa*, 1988
- the various newspapers, magazines and journalists who allowed us to use their cuttings
- photographs given freely by *The Argus*, Obed Zilwa of the *Cape Times* and the United States Information Service
- editing time far beyond contractual requirements from Dene Smuts and Shauna Westcott
- in-depth research by, in particular, Margaret Nash and Shauna Westcott

While every effort has been made to trace and acknowledge copyright holders, this has not always been possible. Should any infringement have occurred, apologies are tendered, and any omissions will be rectified in the event of a reprint.

PREFACE

The value of nonviolent action as a powerful tool for social and political change has been recorded as far back as ancient Rome. In this century, it was developed and refined by Gandhi, who transformed it into an active and dynamic technique that could be politically effective on a large scale. In the 1950s, the American Civil Rights struggles under the inspirational leadership of Martin Luther King depended upon nonviolent action both philosophically and strategically. And in the 1980s, the people of the Philippines overturned an oppressive government through an astonishing and courageous array of nonviolent tactics.

Nonviolent action is not passive resistance – it is what it says it is, action that is nonviolent. Martin Luther King found it to be a mobilising and empowering force, to the extent that even when a struggle is lost, there are gains at the personal and group level. He writes of his own experience in the Deep South:

> The nonviolent approach does not immediately change the heart of the oppressor. It first does something to the hearts and souls of those committed to it. It gives them new self-respect; it calls up resources of strength and courage that they did not know they had. Finally it reaches the opponent and so stirs his conscience that reconciliation becomes a reality.
> (Coretta Scott King, *The Words of Martin Luther King Jnr*, London, Robson Books Ltd, 1984.)

In South Africa too, nonviolent action has a rich history studded with heroic figures, innovative tactics and high ideals. Names that have resonated into the history books span the decades from Luthuli in the 1950s to Tutu in the 1980s and 90s, and embrace the ordinary people who have discovered its power. This book seeks to document some of that history. In doing so, it becomes clear that there is widespread support in South Africa for nonviolent action, amounting to what Walter Wink describes as "probably the largest grassroots eruption of diverse nonviolent strategies in a single struggle in human history!" (Walter Wink, *Jesus' Third Way*, Johannesburg, SACC, 1987.)

That this book is now a reality fulfils a vision that was conceived in the mid-1980s at the Centre for Intergroup Studies. It grew out of a commitment to nonviolence that is the cornerstone of the Centre's work as a facilitator of communication in political and community conflict. Its compilation and publication, and the organisation of the consultative workshop referred to below, were made possible by donations from the Friedrich Ebert Stiftung to whom the Centre is very grateful.

Crucial in shaping the book was the workshop convened in 1988 to create a forum for discussion about its content. Twenty-six informed and committed activists from a range of organisations attended. The consensus was that the book should be a history rather than a polemic, that it should document rather than preach, and that it should not be judgemental of other forms of struggle. The editors have tried to abide by this consensus.

The title emerged as graffiti in September 1989 when, at the height of the Defiance Campaign, the police sprayed purple dye on marchers in Cape Town bearing placards around the theme "The people shall govern". As a slogan, 'The Purple Shall Govern" became a symbol of the campaign, and within the framework of this book, its popularity testified to the powerful voice of nonviolent action. The story is told on page 13 under the heading *Activism*.

The historical perspective of this book should not be interpreted as placing the need for nonviolent action in the past tense. Conflict is a natural and necessary dynamic in every society, and as South Africa leaves apartheid behind and searches for a new dispensation, conflict and violence are, and will continue to be, a stark reality. How that conflict and violence are handled is the question.

Professor H W van der Merwe
Director
Centre for Intergroup Studies
Cape Town, January 1991

INTRODUCTION

When Nelson Mandela paid homage to Martin Luther King and Mahatma Gandhi during his triumphal tours of the USA and India in 1990, he acknowledged a political philosophy – nonviolence – which saw a remarkable resurgence in South Africa in the late 1980s.

Mandela had spent a quarter of a century in prison for espousing armed struggle after 1960. But the ANC was conceived in peace, and born as a mass movement through nonviolent action. The Defiance of Unjust Laws Campaign of 1952, which saw ANC membership grow from 7 000 to 100 000, was a classic example of passive resistance, characterised by politeness, preparation and discipline.

The two historic strands of struggle, violent and nonviolent, were operating simultaneously at the time of the Defiance Campaign of 1989. When nonviolent action coexists with a declared policy of armed struggle, it cannot approach Gandhian refinement and control. But, with violence on the ground and with the ambiguous goals of negotiation or takeover, nonviolent action in South Africa in the late 1980s – the hunger strikes that ended the mass use of the system of detention without trial, the beach protests that showed up the injustice of segregation and the outrageousness of police action – operated on the same premises Martin Luther King described in his *Letter from Birmingham Jail*:

"Why direct action? Why sit-ins, marches and so forth? Isn't negotiation a better path? . . . Indeed this is the very purpose of direct action (which) seeks to create such a crisis and foster such tension that a community which has constantly refused to negotiate is forced to confront this issue."

When the Defiance Campaign culminated in wave upon wave of peace marches, starting in Cape Town in September 1989, the state of emergency was neutralised and nonviolent action achieved a moral victory comparable with that of King's 200 000-strong march on Washington in 1963 which ushered in the Civil Rights Act and led him to say, on receiving the Nobel Peace Prize:

"Negroes in the US, following the people of India, have demonstrated that nonviolence is not sterile passivity, but a powerful and moral force which makes for social transformation."

The capacity for social transformation demonstrated by white South Africa during the peace marches in 1989 appeared to be absent in 1960, the year the ANC and the PAC were banned. The great Cape Town march by 30 000 workers on March 30 that year, which formed part of the PAC's pass campaign, took place days after the Sharpeville shootings and marked the arrival of an era of violent repression and violent revolt. But if the ability to change seemed absent, so was any perception of a moral force at work. Whites felt threatened and excluded. When terror rather than tension is fostered by both or either side, conversion cannot occur.

By contrast, the shooting of Black Consciousness-inspired Sowetan schoolchildren peacefully protesting against Afrikaans instruction in 1976 sent shockwaves travelling through the white community and may well have set in motion the gradual moral shift which eventually made President F W de Klerk's reign possible. Gandhi used to say that his opponent, the British, had the breadth of spirit to be receptive to the moral pressure of satyagraha. President De Klerk provided the equivalent component in South Africa, and nonviolent action finally triumphed.

Nonviolent actions after Soweto 1976 and especially under the state of emergency seemed few and far between, a candle flame obliterated by the flare of battle in strife-torn townships. But the spark of freedom Chief Luthuli asked his followers to keep alive was in fact burning bravely: the range of nonviolent responses shown, from rent boy-cotts to funeral orations was unusually rich. Basing research on Gene Sharp's classic, *The Methods of Nonviolent Action*, and using his categorisation of nonviolence into protest and persuasion, non-cooperation, and intervention, nonviolent acts were col-lected into an alphabet, a lexicon of nonviolence designed to make readers fully literate in the philosophy. As 1989 unfolded, the last letter fell into place: the X factor, the unex-pected ending, began to shape itself. South Africans started to say "Yes" and Zabalaza, "the struggle" for negotiation came to a close with the announcement on 2 February 1990 that the liberation movements were unbanned and Nelson Mandela was to be released.

It is fitting that the first apartheid law to be repealed in 1990 was the Separate Ameni-ties Act, introduced in 1953 after the Courts upheld the right of a black man, George Lusu, to refuse to vacate the "European" waiting room at Cape Town Station. The philosophy of passive resistance was born on a South African station as a result of early colonial segregation. The young lawyer Gandhi, newly qualified in Britain, refused to move from a first class compartment on a train travelling to Pretoria and was evicted at Pietermaritzburg. That night, shivering with cold and humiliation, he resolved to eradi-cate injustice, and to do so by suffering for justice. The mass marches he mobilised here set in motion an historical tide that swept right around the world until, nearly a hundred years later, the wave broke on the South African shores where it had started.

The symbolic South African marches of 1989 were not the only ones that contributed to settlement. The collapse of communism after the people of Eastern Europe took to the streets was one of the many factors, some local, some foreign, that forced the stale-mate that precipitated peace talks.

But although it represented only one of the factors that forced acceptance of the idea of a negotiated settlement, the point that must be made about nonviolent action in South Africa is that it worked, whereas violence did not, not on either side.

The legacy of violence lived on in South Africa in 1990. Ten deaths a day bore grim witness to the difficulty of eradicating a culture allowed to root itself over decades. The deaths won no-one any victories, but the waste went on.

Nonviolence went on working. As pre-negotiation talks between political leaders began, public confession and forgiveness by church leaders demonstrated the depth of the power of moral persuasion. Despite the imperfections of nonviolent action when used alongside violence, nonviolent struggle in South Africa has penetrated the spiritual level which Gandhi considered integral to satyagraha. And of all the good signs that not just settlement but true reconciliation is possible, this is the clearest. A counterculture of nonviolence is establishing itself in South Africa, regenerating from roots that go deep, to the heart of the country.

Dene Smuts, Cape Town, December 1990

Courtesy of OBED ZILWA, CAPE TIMES

LEFT:

Purple rain . . . On 2 September 1989 a protest march in Burg Street, Cape Town, was broken up by police using purple dye sprayed from a Casspir. One lone resister jumped on the roof of the Casspir, grabbed the nozzle attached to the hose, and turned the jet of purple water on to the police. Soon after that grafitti appeared on walls in the city and even on the inside of a police van, which read: "The purple shall govern."

11

ACTIVISM

In nonviolent revolutions against authoritarian rule in many countries, a moment of popular uprising was reached when people shook off their sense of powerlessness and began to act. Individuals not normally involved in struggle redefined their role and identified with – and as – "the people". In South Africa as in South America and Eastern Europe, they included religious leaders, artists and professionals. And here, as in Eastern Europe, they took to the streets in the late 1980s.

■ PURPLE REIGN

YOU might be forgiven for thinking that Cape Town's police force has a wry sense of humour. Friday's *Weekly Mail* Classifieds carried the advert: "You know who you are. You are beautiful and delicious. Meet me in Greenmarket Square at 11am on Saturday." Saturday morning you can hardly move amongst the fleamarket stalls for the men and women in blue.

Every corner holds a crowd of policemen struggling for pavement space. Suspicious security branch types sporting anoraks slouch against the windows of the coffee shops and mutter into walkie-talkies.

MDM marshalls face the unenviable task of identifying potential marchers milling on Greenmarket Square and ushering them into a nearby church hall from where the march will begin.

Inside I can hardly believe that a church hall can be so full and small and tense. People are sitting three to a chair and overflowing on to the floor. We are asked to be patient as our "head marshall" waits for a message from St George's Cathedral where another march waits to begin. Marches are due to leave from different venues aiming to divide the energies of the people.

The theme of the march is "The people shall govern". We intend to march to parliament in arm-linked rows of eight behind our chosen dignitaries and representatives. If the police order us to disperse, we will sit down or kneel in the road. Kneel in the road? Nothing on earth will persuade me to kneel on the road in front of a serious mean-looking police force. My stomach contracts with fear and doubt. I look around and see my own expression on other faces and I am temporarily reassured.

Walking out of the church into Burg Street is like the moment before jumping from a high place. All of us know exactly what is outside. I hope that all the others are braver than me. There's still time to pull out. The rows are forming and my elbow forms a link. Figuratively, we close our eyes and take deep breaths and launch ourselves forward. The crowd of Saturday morning spectators is huge, the pavements are spilling over with curious shoppers. At the end of the road, the police are six deep and waiting. I see no quirts or batons. I wonder what they have in store for us. Will we just be led right through the phalanx of policemen? Predictably, our march grinds to a halt as we are given ten minutes to disperse.

The whole march sits down in the road and the tension mounts as our leaders negotiate with the police to continue to parliament. The crowd of supporters is clapping slowly and cheering.

Now we see what the ten minutes was all about. The yellow pride of Caledon Square careens down the road flashing its lights. A soft noise of hydraulics and the nozzle of the infamous water cannon is aimed at the crowd. The marchers brace themselves. Somewhere a crucial button is pushed and a sharp jet of water bursts forth, changing in mid-stream to lurid purple.

Some are hit head on, full in the face. Some are knocked off their knees. Scramble and panic and somebody is shouting "Sit down, sit down". Some are pinned against the wall and are painted like paper dolls as the jet sweeps past. A small remaining huddle in the road are covering their heads under the purple spray.

The supply of purple dye seems endless and the machine sprays on and on. The gutters run with oily foam. The crowd is stunned into strange silence. All we can do is watch this weird purple blast sweep backwards and forwards. The church facade is transformed in strange slow motion from grey to psychedelic in a flourish of the jet. It seems as if it will never end.

Then it stops.

A lone protester has climbed on top of the truck and is diverting the nozzle away from the people. He is struggling with it, fighting with it, and the purple jet streaks wildly across the buildings. The crowd stares for a moment in disbelief – then goes wild, cheering, shouting and leaping in the air with delight for this brave young man.

It is an indescribable moment. Even the policemen can only stand and stare seeming to have momentarily lost their grip on the situation.

Not for long. They retaliate as teargas billows into the square. Marchers and policemen alike are stumbling and choking and fighting for breath. Spectators have become participants, willingly or not.

Media reports can't possibly describe the shock and pain of being teargassed – what feels like an acute asthma attack. Some collapse in the road. Eyes streaming, nose and mouth and lungs burning, we run up streets, into buildings, it's like a war.

It is a war, and it feels like the city is on our side.

A friend of mine seeks refuge in a hairdressing salon and is washed clean of his purple stains. Another is rescued by taxi and whisked off down the back streets. A department store is used as a hideout and a comrade emerges with a clean pair of trousers.

We hear that all purple people are being rounded up and arrested. Jackets and jerseys are turned inside out and incriminating stains are quickly concealed.

All the roads have been cordoned off and we walk up the middle of Ádderley Street in a daze. The silence is heavy and ominous. Five hundred people have been arrested and taken to Caledon Square, we hear. Three special courts have been convened to process them. Police still surround St George's Cathedral.

There are still tedious hours of waiting outside the court. As each little group emerges from the dock the crowd claps politely. It's like the aftermath of an earthquake or a wedding. Now there's only cleaning up and counting bruises and suddenly

A lone protester has climbed on top of the truck and is diverting the nozzle away from the people. He is struggling with it, fighting with it, and the purple jet streaks wildly across the buildings. The crowd stares for a moment in disbelief – then goes wild, cheering, shouting and leaping in the air with delight for this brave young man.

discovering you're hungry.

If it was a war, then peaceful protest was the victor. Not a stone was thrown. The feeling of unity and friendship in the city was real and very tangible.

By Monday morning an efficient graffiti artist had said it for all of us: "The purple shall govern". I can believe it.

– Alison Ozinsky, Upfront, November 1989

ADVERTISEMENT

The founding of "alternative" newspapers in SA has given rise to a new genre of advertising. "Alternative" advertising sends messages, asks questions, conveys information, expresses solidarity and outrage: it translates the traditional nonviolent method of protest and persuasion into a modern medium.

■ LISTEN carefully to what the ANC leaders will say at their welcome home rally on Sunday 29 October and judge for yourself whether you should have been prevented from hearing what they and other restricted organisations and people have been saying for the last 30 years.

We call for the immediate abolition of all restrictions which impede freedom of expression.

Anti Censorship Action Group
PO Box 260425, Excom 2023

– Weekly Mail, 27.10.89

■ SOON THERE MAY BE TWO

DOCTOR Ivan Toms is currently serving a 21-month sentence in Pollsmoor Prison for refusing to serve in the SADF.

David Bruce, 24, has also refused to serve in the SADF. His trial commences on July 19 in Johannesburg. He faces up to six years in prison.

How many more must go to jail before conscientious objectors are given real alternatives?

Issued by Objector Support Group, Cape Town

– Weekly Mail, 15.7.88

■ ADVERT CALLS FOR RELEASE OF CHILDREN

AN advertisement calling on the State President, Mr P W Botha, and the Minister of Law and Order, Mr Adriaan Vlok, to release children still in detention under the state of emergency, will appear today in the *Weekend Post*.

As part of the Black Sash's Free the Children Campaign, the advert is signed by 123 local churchleaders, politicians, civil rights campaigners, city councillors, businessmen, lawyers and other concerned citizens.

Among the signatories are Bishop Michael Coleman, Roman Catholic Bishop of the PE diocese; Bishop Bruce Evans, Bishop of the PE diocese of the Anglican Church; Rev George Irvine, head of the Methodist Church in the Eastern Cape; Mrs Valerie Hunt, director of the School Feeding Fund; Mr John Malcomess, PFP MP for PE Central; Mr Andrew Savage, PFP MP for Walmer; Mr Athol Fugard, playwright; and Mr Tony Gilson, director of the PE Chamber of Commerce.

– EP Herald, 20.12.86

■ A LEGAL friend of mine was hard pressed to keep a straight face when a very sweet but altogether too earnest visitor to onse land inquired after the health of a certain detainee. "Has Caroline Cullinan been released yet?" he asked, with great concern. "Caroline Cullinan?" my friend replied. "I had no idea she had been detained." Oh yes, the visitor twanged. The Weekly Mail, he said, has been campaigning for her release by publishing a Free Caroline Cullinan calendar.

– Weekly Mail, 24.11.89

South African and multi-national corporations have adopted the new genre for their corporate image/social responsibility advertisements in "alternative" publications. One in particular has so diligently adapted the message to the medium that it must take the credit for a whole new visual style.

■ THERE is much confusion about the latest advertisement from everyone's favourite multinational, Shell.

Erudite Cape Town artist Nicolaas Vergunst says not only is the picture adapted from a 1926 Soviet poster by Adolf Strakhov (original slogan: "You are a free woman – help to build socialism") but the text is adopted from the Congress Alliance's 1955 Freedom Charter: "Everyone has the right to vote for all law-making bodies."

"Both picture and slogan originate from mass-based struggles for socialist democracy," says Nicolaas, "so what is this piece of promotional propaganda about?" Has Shell suddenly become convinced of the merits of a socialist future, he wonders.

– Weekly Mail, 19.2.88

The stark "socialist" look has since been used with great effect by the Chamber of Mines in print media as well as on TV, where mine workers are so rendered as to appear simultaneously austere and glamorous.

Shell has continued its bold campaign without visuals but often retaining the sparse "Charter" style, for example "All children have the right to peace and progress", while other advertisements are reminiscent of demand lists issued by anti-apartheid organisations:

"Free the democratic process. Shell urges government to:

1. End the state or emergency
2. Release and unban all political leaders
3. Lift restrictions on democratic organisations
4. Allow and encourage freedom of expression."

AFFIDAVIT

Under conditions of repression and censorship such as those prevailing in SA especially during the state of emergency, affidavits, or statements given under oath, offered a means of making the kind of facts researched and reported by the press in free societies part of the public record.

In November 1984, the South African Catholic Bishops' Conference used affidavits and interviews as the basis for a book on *Police Conduct During Township Protests, August – November 1984*. The American Lawyers' Committee for Human Rights also used affidavits for their study, *The War Against Children: South Africa's Youngest Victims* (New York, 1986).

The late Molly Blackburn and Di Bishop, both members of the Black Sash and MPCs at the time, visited Eastern Cape towns between 1982 and 1985 to record events in this way.

In 1986, after KTC squatter camp was attacked and burned, a combined UCT Department of Criminology and Legal Resources Centre team helped KTC residents make thousands of affidavits for a damages action against the Minister of Law and Order. Affidavits used in court cases serve the secondary purpose of informing the public when they are reported. After December 1986, the SA media was prohibited from publishing affidavits filed in court cases involving emergency regulation detainees until judgment was given.

An affidavit made on death row by Almond Butana Nofomela led to exposure of the CCB when ex-captain Dirk Coetzee, named by Nofomela, told his story to *Vrye Weekblad* before fleeing the country.

See also: Court action, Information, Publishing, Witness

ALTERNATIVE STRUCTURES

"Our time has witnessed the emergence of a new historical phenomenon: the 'National Security State', a colossus of surveillance and repressive might made virtually impregnable as a result of the wizardry of military and electronic technology. Such a colossus should deprive us of all hope," writes American theologian Walter Wink.

"But the paradoxical consequence is just the opposite. Since armed resistance is largely futile, people have taken recourse in nonviolent means . . . . Because anti-apartheid leaders are arrested almost as soon as they emerge, resistance groups have invented non-hierarchical and democratic organisational forms. Means and ends coalesce as people create for themselves social instruments for change that already embody the better life they seek ahead."

Writing on such alternative institutions in his classic, *The Methods of Nonviolent Action*, Gene Sharp notes: "When their creation and growth produces a challenge to the previous institutions, the new ones constitute nonviolent intervention.

"Schools seem to be one of the most common social institutions for parallel development. During the German occupation of their country, Polish citizens set up an education system independent of Nazi control. In 1942 in the Warsaw district alone more than 85 000 children were receiving education in small secret sessions in private homes. Over 1 700 had by that date been graduated from high school, receiving innocently worded cards which were after the war to be exchanged for official diplomas.

"In addition to privately teaching slaves and free negroes to read and write, abolitionists and others before the American Civil War sometimes established new schools, usually for negroes but sometimes for an integrated enrolment. In many states, both such private instruction and schools were forbidden by law. In breaking up a school for slaves, a grand jury in Lexington, Kentucky, argued that the school would enlighten 'the minds of those whose happiness obviously depends on their ignorance'."

In SA, student representative councils and PTSAs on which students, staff and parents are represented, the National Education Crisis Committee (NECC) and its successors are examples of an attempt to create alternative structures. The NECC was responsible for publishing the resource manual *What Is History?* as part of a process of developing alternative education programmes.

Co-operatives, community clinics, legal resource centres and advice offices all offer alternatives where existing social institutions fail to meet citizens' needs.

An example is the Organisation for Appropriate Social Services in South Africa (Oassa), founded in the Transvaal in 1983. A Cape branch began in 1985 and by 1988 there were branches in Durban and Pietermaritzburg.

Oassa's work includes providing medical and psychological help to released detainees and other victims of state-imposed suffering and stress.

Street committees and area committees are examples of alternative local government as well as a response to the banning and arrest of black leaders. People's courts – in which the local community deals with disputes and crime – are another alternative structure. Such courts, where ordinary people take turns to serve as officials, became part of the justice system of Mozambique after independence. In SA "kangaroo courts" have often themselves been guilty of violent action but there is documented evidence that people's courts serve a useful social function.

Street and area committees have been described as sophisticated forms of democratic organisation – and many were. But it is important not to idealise them, Steven Friedman argued in *Die Suid-Afrikaan* in August 1989.

Resistance was well organised in some townships during the 1984/86 period, but in others it was anarchic – and undemocratic. Some street committees "consisted of small bands of activists who appointed themselves" and violence was often used "to impose the will of groups of activists on entire communities".

Friedman notes that "men like Mkhuseli Jack of Port Elizabeth and Gugile Nkwinti of Port Alfred who relied on organisation and negotiation faced pressure from violent youth groups who saw them as 'too moderate', and that one of the purposes behind developing democratic structures was to bring militant youths under control."

Not all activists supported the claims, common at the time, that "township conflict would create 'liberated zones' which would become beachheads for an assault on the state". The difference between the advocates of organisation (towards negotiation) and mobilisation (making townships "ungovernable") was real. "More patient strategies have gained ground partly because the 'revolution' failed, not because it did not happen at all," Friedman says.

■ STREET-STYLE DEMOCRACY – CRADOCK ACTIVIST SPEAKS

CRADOCK put street committees on the map last year. Why do you see them as an important form of organisation?

If the street committees had not taken up the reins of organisation during the state of emergency I'm quite sure Cradora would have died.

But when the leadership was detained, the street committees were already in place, and our networks were running smoothly.

When you have structures like these, detentions of individuals can't destroy you. They would have to detain 500 people in Cradock alone to put a stop to these structures. So mass participation is our best defence.

We had also already adapted to meetings being banned, and to using the street committees to establish mass majority feeling on issues, and to make sure everyone was up to date. But they harassed people about the street committees in detention, which caused some people to take fright.

What kind of issues are dealt with in the street committees?

The street committees discuss community issues like the consumer boycott, but decisions are made at the level of the township as a whole, once the view from all the streets has been gauged.

Then they also discuss issues like basic hygiene, e.g. how to wash babies, and issues of morality. So, if a youngster is giving problems because of liquor, the street committee can speak to him. But if he doesn't listen, it must go to the area committee.

Or if the street is very dirty, full of litter, the street committee can decide that this weekend the youth will clean the street; or this weekend the fathers are all going to collect their spades and wheelbarrows to mend the holes in the road.

And Cradora acts on general grievances that emerge – like the corruption with the pensions.

Very old people were waiting all day in all weather and having to give bribes to get their money, while some elements were able to push in the queue.

So Cradora went there and ensured these old people were properly accommodated, and that people got to the counter on a first come, first served, basis.

We also educated them about their rights as pensioners while they waited.

– Saspu National, February 1986

Not all activists supported the claims, common at the time, that township conflict would create "liberated zones" which would become beachheads for an assault on the state. The difference between the advocates of organisation (towards negotiation) and mobilisation (making townships "ungovernable") was real.

19

■ PEOPLE'S COURTS IN CHARGE

THE anarchy is over in Atteridgeville – 12 people's courts see to that.

The courts, set up by the Atteridgeville-Saulsville Resident's Association (ASRO) in a bid to end the chaos in the streets, have gained control of township affairs.

Overseeing the court affairs is an advice office which serves as a "court of appeal". The courts were set up after the escalation of the war between police and community councillors on the one hand, and residents on the other.

During the war, numerous youths died in attacks on their homes – attacks which were blamed on "the system". Community councillors' and policemen's homes were petrol-bombed, and several more youths died in what were described as "retaliatory raids".

The local town council was virtually rendered inoperative and many residents stopped reporting cases to the police.

Initially, the response from the youth was to set up their own form of justice. But, in their bid to uproot "criminal elements", they used extremely violent punishment.

The residents were angered by this and decided to stamp out the "kangaroo courts". It was then that the people's courts were born.

ASRO set up its own courts under control of its area committees. The courts hear charges ranging from assault, crimen injuria, theft, and civil cases such as matrimonial disputes and disobedience.

– New Nation, 13.2.86

■ MEET ME DOWN AT MANDELA PARK

THERE is Oliver Tambo Park in White City, Sisulu Park in Orlando West, Nelson Mandela Park and Steve Biko Park in Mohlakeng near Randfontein.

The parks began when essential township services, like the removal of refuse, began suffering because of unrest. Residents started dumping their refuse at street corners and in any available open space.

Within days there were mounds of filth, posing a health threat and becoming an eye-sore. Groups of youths soon organised themselves to do something about it. Using tools "borrowed" from the family toolbox, they went about clearing debris from the streets and open spaces.

It soon became a mammoth task, with grader and tipper-truck drivers "requested" to shift mounds of dirt and move loads of soil.

Motorists and taxi-owners were asked to put some coins in empty beer cans held by those whose hands are too weak to handle a spade. The money was used to buy food for the crew, paint and other neccesities.

This type of action caught the eyes of environmentalists who donated trees and other shrubbery.

At the Mandela and Biko parks in Randfontein there were busts of the two leaders. But before the parks could be officially opened, the busts were smashed and the parks destroyed.

This has only served to make the youth more determined to build parks. They are springing up all over – in Mamelodi, Witbank, Bekkersdal, Middelburg, Atteridgeville and Natalspruit.

– Weekly Mail, 7.2.86

There is Oliver Tambo Park in White City, Sisulu Park in Orlando West, Nelson Mandela Park and Steve Biko Park in Mohlakeng near Randfontein . . . .

■ ALEX ACTIVISTS ARE BACK ON THE STREETS

THE Alexandra Action Committee (AAC) is back on the streets again.

The committee, led by trade unionist Moses Mayekiso, is spearheading a township clean-up campaign which began at the weekend.

The AAC is back in action after three years, following the lengthy treason trial of its members, including Mayekiso. The five were acquitted earlier this year.

According to a statement by Mayekiso after the event: "The whole of Alexandra township was full of activity for the first time since early 1986, when all such activities were clamped down upon."

It seems the AAC can still count on the support of the Alexandra residents. More than 3 000 people participated in the clean-up, which was supported by the Alexandra Youth Congress and Alexandra Student Congress.

This follows the failure two weeks earlier of a clean-up campaign called by the Alexandra town council. Residents believe the call by the council was intended to pre-empt the action of the AAC. But residents ignored the council's campaign.

On Saturday people piled refuse from backyards and hostels in front of their gates and on street corners, which was later collected by refuse trucks organised by the AAC.

People sang as they cleaned – undeterred by the presence of the security forces. Members of the SADF and police monitored the proceedings, filming with video cameras.

– Weekly Mail, 28.7.89

See also: Camouflage, Underground

ANNIVERSARIES

Anniversaries can serve as rallying points around which campaigns and other nonviolent action is built. For instance, on March 21 1986, church bells were rung and vigils held in memory of the 69 pass law protesters shot by police at Sharpeville in 1960, and the 21 mourners killed by police at a funeral in Langa, Uitenhage, exactly 25 years later.

On February 14 1988, the people of Mogopa gathered to observe the fourth anniversary of their forced removal by the SADF. Women who sang for the gathering wore sackcloth, the Biblical symbol of loss and grief.

Among the dates popularly observed in South Africa is June 16 or Soweto Day, the anniversary of the beginning of the 1976 uprising. Campaigns for recognition of this anniversary have caused many businesses and institutions to treat June 16 as a paid holiday.

■ MAY 1 IS OUR DAY – AND ALWAYS WILL BE

PW Botha says:

The first Friday of every May is "Workers' Day" – a public holiday.

Cosatu says:

No thanks. You can't give us what we have already won.

May Day is ours. May 1 is ours. We had it last year. We had it this year. And we'll have it again next year – our workers' holiday.

This country's employers have recognised that May Day is ours. It is written into agreements affecting hundreds of thousands of workers.

So what is this "first Friday every May"? Who did you consult? Who gave you the mandate? We never raised the demand.

We said May Day was ours. We told employers it was something we could not give up.

And we won't.

– Cosatu News, No 5, 1987

See also: Campaign, Homage

AUSTERITY

Austerity is often part of religious practice, for instance during Lent or Ramadan. Activists in SA have observed austerity to deepen commitment and to show others the seriousness of that commitment. Examples are the "Black Christmas" of 1976 and the 1986 "Christmas Against the Emergency". Austerity can also have a side-effect: giving up luxuries can affect traders' bank balances.

■ CHRISTMAS CAMPAIGN BLASTS OFF, SAYS UDF

THE "Christmas Against the Emergency" campaign has captured the public's imagination and is the "talk of the townships", according to UDF publicity secretary Murphy Morobe.

The 10-day campaign for an end to the emergency has won support from a wide spectrum of people in the townships, ranging from clergymen, through taxi owners to sportsmen, Morobe said.

The campaign aims to draw people into dignified, nonviolent action for the lifting of the state of emergency, the release of political prisoners and detainees,

PAUL WEINBERG

LEFT
May Day – an important date on the workers' calendar – is celebrated by Cosatu members at a rally in 1986.

particularly children, and the unbanning of the African National Congress.

The UDF has offered "guidelines" as to how opposition to the emergency should be symbolised over the Christmas season, starting on December 16 and ending on December 26.

The guidelines include lighting candles every night between 7 and 9, singing Nkosi Sikelel' iAfrika, reciting a special unity pledge and observing silence for one minute.

The campaign will open with the ringing of church bells at 6am on December 16.

Morobe said: "The response has been positive. Shebeens have agreed to close at 8pm over the ten-day period and to display the unity pledge prominently."

– *Weekly Mail, 12.12.86*

See also: Hunger strike, Sacrifice, Satyagraha

BOYCOTT

The word boycott was first used in Ireland in 1880 by peasants and traders who ostracised a Captain CC Boycott, land agent for the Earl of Erne, after he refused to reduce rents. Primarily a method of non-cooperation, boycotts can also constitute intervention.

Three forms of boycott operating on an international level have had the express aim of isolating SA: cultural, academic and sports boycotts. The first two have been particularly controversial.

■ CENSORSHIP OR STRATEGY?

THE first salvo in the boycott debate was fired when the former "priest of Sophiatown", Father Trevor Huddleston, pleaded for cultural sanctions in the London *Observer* in October 1954. "I am pleading for a cultural boycott of SA. I am asking those who believe racialism to be sinful or wrong to refuse to encourage it by accepting any engagement to act, to perform as a musical artist or as a ballet dancer – in short, to engage in any contacts which would provide entertainment for any one section of the community."

In 1956, the British actors' union Equity decided that its members would not perform before segregated audiences. In 1957 the British Musicians Union (BMU) followed suit. After intervention by the BMU, the Rolling Stones cancelled an SA tour planned for 1964. Since 1963, prominent playwrights have refused to allow their work to be performed before segregated audiences.

On December 2 1968, the UN General Assembly accepted resolution 2396, in terms of which all member states and organisations were asked to cut "cultural, educational and sporting ties with the racist regime and with organisations and institutions in SA practising apartheid".

On December 16 1980 a "Register of Artists, Actors and Others who have performed in SA" and a "Register of Sports Contact" were established in terms of UN resolution 35/206E. The register, colloquially known as the "blacklist", was largely based on newspaper reports. The Special Committee Against Apartheid was responsible for implementing it. Performances by well-known artists have been banned in certain countries on the grounds of their presence in the register. The Swedish ban on superstar Frank Sinatra was perhaps the most celebrated. After his Sun City performance he had to leave Sweden amid huge protest action without a single appearance. Cliff Richard was allowed to perform in Norway only after promising in writing that he would not play again in SA.

In the most recent edition of the register, under the sub-heading "Deletions", Sinatra's name appears with, among others, Boney M, Joe Dolan, Shirley Bassey, Black Sabbath, The Fortunes, Marmelade, Cher, Eartha Kitt, the Bellamy Brothers, the Vienna Boys' Choir and Status Quo.

The effect of the boycott cannot be underestimated. Any sports fan will be able to confirm the far-reaching consequences of cultural, sport and academic sanctions. The isolation of SA sport is the most comprehensive of all sanctions but on a cultural level the isolation is also striking: leading artists avoid SA.

Subtle but important changes in the boycott strategy have begun to develop recently . . . . The turning point was the 1987 Graceland tour of Paul Simon, Ray Phiri, Ladysmith Black Mambaso, Hugh Masekela and Miriam Makeba. While the British Anti-Apartheid Movement was acting in terms of the letter of UN resolution 2396 and making life unbearable for the touring group, the ANC in London was more tolerant. Serious tensions developed and the differences were overcome only when ANC president Oliver Tambo declared in May 1987 that the changing situation in SA, the intensifying resistance, had to lead also to modifications in the cultural boycott.

Cultural productions, structures and artists had developed in resistance which, it was argued, should be supported and nurtured rather than boycotted.

At the same time within SA the UDF was formulating criteria for tours and visits to SA: exemption from the boycott could be obtained only if the visit was approved by the internal democratic movement and by its overseas allies; in addition, the visit or tour had to further the national democratic struggle for a non-racial SA. . . .

The cultural boycott, initiated purely as a sanction, now developed a constructive element: support for the developing alternative culture. Another shift was that responsibility for the practical implementation of the boycott moved largely from the external anti-apartheid movement to internal resistance organisations.

According to the May 1989 ANC statement, democratic values should be supported and encouraged, contact with democratic cultural workers in the rest of the world should be extended. This includes the dissemination of books, newspapers, magazines, films and tapes from abroad – the kind of information that, according to the statement, subverts the misanthropic goals of apartheid.

In tandem with renewed political resistance, the last few years have seen the development of various new anti-apartheid organisations in the sporting, academic and cultural arenas. The National Sports Congress (NSC), the Union of Democratic University Staff Associations (Udusa), the National Education Crisis Committee (NECC), the Film and Allied Workers Organisation (Fawo), the Congress of SA Writers and South African Music Alliance (Sama) have – beyond their common anti-apartheid position - comparable attitudes to the cultural boycott and the national democratic struggle.

– Hein Willemse, *Die Suid-Afrikaan, October 1989*

Inside SA, boycott was the weapon of resistance used to reorganise itself. The campaign for a boycott of elections for the new tricameral parliament in 1984 was the campaign on which the newly founded UDF cut its teeth. Many people did not register as a way of protesting against the new constitution, while 80% of registered voters stayed away on polling day, removing the facade of legitimacy decisively.

The rent boycott which began in the Vaal Triangle in August 1984, spreading nationally to 50 townships by September 1986, is perhaps the most widespread and sustained form of economic non-cooperation ever mounted in SA.

In September 1986, the Community Research Group at Wits University estimated that 60% of the total black township population was not paying rent, costing local authorities R1 million a day.

By the end of 1988, Soweto residents owed an officially estimated R186,5 million in arrears. By the end of 1989 the government was ready to abandon coercion - and the Soweto City Council - and to negotiate. MDM leaders were ready too, with research to back up the broad political and economic basis of their claims.

■ THE EMPIRE STRIKES BACK

AUGUST 27, 1986, White City residents clashed with municipal police and the army. 27 people died. Stories circulated like wildfire. Many said that armed ANC cadres had ambushed the police. Some said that local youths had been warned that evictions were to take place, and had prepared caches of stones to fight.

A few months later, the scene was almost repeated in Phomolong. Someone blew the "help" whistle and out came innocent tenants, thinking it was a genuine cry. Four died that night.

Came 1987, there was still uncertainty. People started to receive electricity and water bills only, with no rent statements. Evictions increased. There would be new rumours every few weeks, about different townships – now Emndeni, now Naledi, now Zola. At that point street committees were no longer functioning because leaders had been detained. There was no longer any co-ordination between the people and the comrades. People ceased to think in terms of street committees, and, one by one, they started paying. No one would publicly admit to be paying rent, but it was obvious that many were. People gave all sorts of excuses for being seen at the offices.

Chiawello residents received letters informing them that the rent issue was under review and tenants would be hearing from the council soon. This gave residents hope. But nothing more happened. People did not know how much they were owing. Main roads acquired billboards which even to this day still read: "Water is a bargain, but even bargains must be paid for". The same was said of electricity, housing and transport. The inference was that residents do not want to pay, while what we want is to solve the problem so that we can pay.

People became angry about the "bargain" advertisements, because water and electricity bills are astronomical. They are much higher than for white homes, and the story is that we pay more per unit because the white areas have already paid off their infrastructure.

Besides, since the riots started in 1985 there has been no meter reader. How do they arrive at the figures?

Came 1988, we welcomed the year with hope. People prayed the rent issue would be resolved. Then the Soweto Council started cracking the whip. They evicted people in certain areas of Chiawello 1 and 2 most of whom were pensioners. One was left out in the cold for the night and has since died of the exposure. Then one bright summer morning in Chiawello 3, residents were rudely awoken. There was a contingent. They wanted rent.

The soldiers stood pointing their rifles while officials demanded the rent receipt. People mumbled a promise and were told the soldiers would be back the following Thursday and woe betide defaulters.

Some residents rushed to pay or make a pledge to pay. Came the fatal Thursday and the officials kept their promise. Those who did not have current receipts had their furniture thrown into the army trucks and their homes locked up. People were running backwards and forwards looking for leaders, looking for money, pointing fingers at those who were not raided.

Streets were piled with televisions, sofas, fridges, food. Women wailed hopelessly. Children watched their beds being flung into trucks. The constables loaded, under the watch of the soldiers, casually chomping at the fruits or sipping drinks from the fridge. The sound of splintering and cracking rings out. Drawers fall out of cupboards, and clothes and cutlery fall out of drawers.

By evening there was chaos. The township was divided. Some had paid, some wanted to pay but had no money, some demanded solidarity in the name of the original Chiawello issue. Others demanded solidarity in the name of the big political issue.

– Nomavenda Mathiane, *Frontline, February 1988*

■ A FLURRY OF MEETINGS AS RENTS CRISIS FLARES

MEMBERS of the Soweto People's Delegation (SPD) – formed last year to represent residents on the rent issue – staged a series of residents' meetings in the giant township at the weekend to reiterate demands for the scrapping of residents' R200-million rent backlog.

The meetings followed a controversial statement by Soweto Mayor Sam Mkhwanazi last week that arrears would be frozen rather than scrapped. Earlier reports that he had promised to write off unpaid rents had misquoted him, he claimed.

At the SPD meetings, civic leaders such as Frank Chikane, Lebamang Sebidi and Albertina Sisulu reiterated that the rent boycott would not be called off until the Soweto City Council addressed their demands.

In addition to the scrapping of rent and service arrears, these include demands for a single, open Johannesburg-Soweto metropolis, that rented houses be given to tenants, and that better services be provided at cheaper tariffs.

If the Soweto City Council should not agree on a response, SPD members said they would take the issue and their arguments to the Johannesburg City Council, the Transvaal Provincial Administration and the Department of Constitutional Development and Planning.

The findings of a Planact report commissioned by the SPD have considerably weakened the moral position of the authorities, and may help reshape urban politics by showing for the first time how black Sowetans are subsidising the cash-rich Johannesburg City Council. The report argues that the unification of the Soweto and Johannesburg tax base is the only lasting solution to the fiscal crisis in the townships.

Among the report's findings are that about 280 000 Sowetans, 96% of the township's employed population, contribute their labour power to the Johannesburg economy and that Sowetans spend R1 billion in Johannesburg's central

If the legal protest marches sweeping the country in late 1989 represented the beginnings of a climate for negotiation, discussions between Sowetan leaders and the TPA were the start of actual talks.

business district. The report points out that 70% of Johannesburg's income, accruing from service charges, comes from businesses.

"It is black labour and black consumption expenditure that are the foundations of the businesses, contributing no less than 74% of the council's assessment rates," it notes.

The SPD sees the document as a starting-point for negotiations with the state. "If Chris Heunis says he wants a 'grand indaba', here is the city, here is the report and here is the group," said the delegation's Frank Chikane.

– Weekly Mail, 14.4.89

■ SYMBOLIC MARCHES BUT REAL DEBATE IN SOWETO

THE recent legal protest marches may represent the beginnings of a climate for negotiation. But what may be far more significant is the beginnings of actual negotiation between government officials and extra-parliamentary opposition movements.

Talks this week between the Transvaal Provincial Administration and the Soweto People's Delegation over the future of the township focused on local issues – rents, services, houses and taxes. But they are local issues with national political implications.

Perhaps the most important of these is simply one of power. The TPA has conceded that the SPD is going to have a say in the running of Soweto. This is the equivalent, albeit at local level, of the government saying it cannot have constitutional talks without the extra-parliamentary opposition movements.

While both the SPD and the TPA stressed the common ground between them, the differences – over issues such as rents and taxes – reflect the fact that what is at issue in the talks is fundamental apartheid structures.

The first significant aspect of the talks was who was there and why. The SPD team included Archbishop Desmond Tutu, the Rev Frank Chikane, Cyril Ramaphosa, Albertina Sisulu. On the province side were administrator Danie Hough and his executive committee. Also on the province side were members of the Soweto City Council – as it were, the junior partners in the team.

While province has to give the Soweto council some legitimacy – Hough stressed it was the legally elected body – this week's meeting is evidence of the TPA's realisation that the rent boycott will remain unresolved and the township's finances in crisis unless it negotiates with people who have rather more legitimacy than the council.

– Weekly Mail, 6.10.89

Consumer boycotts have been successful in forcing talks at local level, despite the repeated imprisonment of boycott leaders under emergency regulations that declared boycotts subversive

■ BUYING POWER IS A WEAPON

THE charismatic young leader of the PE Consumer Boycott Committee and the PE Youth Congress, Mkhuseli Jack, is unbanned and the PE boycott resumes on

April 1.

He believes similar nationwide boycotts will force businessmen and the government to the negotiating table.

Hours after a PE court ruled his banning order invalid, 28-year-old Jack told cheering crowds: "Our buying power is going to be the thing that is going to decide the future of our country. We are not going to abandon the consumer boycott until it suits us."

– New Nation, 26.3.86

The Eastern Cape boycott campaign of 1985/86 resulted in historic meetings between black leaders and white business interests.

For instance, in the second week of November 1986, the Port Elizabeth Chamber of Commerce evaded the barbed wire fence surrounding New Brighton to hold a secret meeting with the few boycott leaders not in detention. A week later those leaders had disappeared. According to the Black Sash, over 1 000 PE residents, including boycott leader Mkhuseli Jack, were in detention at that time. *(Weekly Mail,* 21.11.86)

After the commencement of President De Klerk's reforms, boycotts became a anti-segregation tool particularly in Conservative Party-controlled local authority areas, notably in the Transvaal. The Boksburg boycott was an early example.

■ COUNCIL FURY AT BOKSBURG TRADE TURNABOUT

JOHANNESBURG. – Boksburg's businessmen are delighted by the sudden turn of events after President FW de Klerk's announcement that the town's central business district and parts of Reiger Park would become free trading areas.

The Conservative Party-controlled East Rand town was declared an open trading area by President De Klerk last night, a move that has infuriated the council as much as it has delighted retailers, especially Indian traders who will no longer have to hide their business ownership behind white nominees.

The proclamation, promulgated in Pretoria, came as speculation mounted that the government was planning a major move in Boksburg in the wake of a jubilant return last weekend of coloured and black shoppers to the town.

They returned following President De Klerk's announcement of his intention to scrap the Separate Amenities Act.

The business boycott, which resulted in shops closing and many people losing their jobs, took place after the CP-controlled town council imposed petty apartheid regulations on the town shortly after winning the municipal elections there in October last year.

– The Argus, 23.11.89

Consumer boycotts have often been marred by the coercion used to enforce them in the townships. But the gains outweighed the costs, which were borne by those intended to bear them. The same cannot be said for the school boycott.

ass rejection of the Bantu education system came to a head in 1976 as Soweto students marched in protest against the imposition of Afrikaans as a medium of instruction. Author Alan Paton called the protest "the end of an era" and "the day black South Africans finally said to whites: You can't do this to us anymore".

The state responded with force, and police shooting of unarmed students on June 16 provoked country-wide unrest. Over 500 young people were killed, many more were injured and some 5 000 fled the country.

Since then school boycotts have occurred regularly, with 1980 and 1984/85 periods of particularly widespread confrontation between black students and the authorities.

More recently PTSAs, the NECC and UWC have been among those struggling to counter the slogan "liberation before education" popularised in 1986. Archbishop Desmond Tutu and Dr Allan Boesak are among high-profile individuals who have urged students to consider that the school boycott may be a strategy whose costs outweigh present usefulness.

There have been gains – in student awareness, in organisational growth (SRCs, PTSAs), in the development of "people's education", in vastly increased state expenditure on black education.

But costs have been severe – detentions of students, teachers and organisational leaders, dismissal of teachers, lock-outs of students perceived as "trouble-makers", occupation of schools by security forces, student casualties in clashes, increasingly repressive "regulations" for students and teachers, and the widespread deterioration of such educational opportunities as are available. Above all, the culture of learning has collapsed, leaving the vast majority of SA's population ill-equipped – only a third of black matrics passed in 1990 – for the future for which they have fought.

BRIDGE-BUILDING

here societies are divided, social intervention can combat the ignorance, fear and hostility that separation engenders. The life of Molly Blackburn, killed in a car accident in December 1985, is a shining example of the impact an individual can have.

"We salute you comrade Molly" was one of many graffiti in Eastern Cape townships that bore witness to the respect and affection she won. Tens of thousands came to mourn at her funeral.

She once said to her sister Judy Chalmers, also an activist: "White South Africans think that the gap between black and white is too wide to be bridged. I don't think this is so. If you stretch out a loving hand, somewhere on the other side a loving hand will take it and that will be the beginning of a bridge."

Another individual who practised social intervention is Dr Nico Smith, once a theologian at Stellenbosch, who became a minister in the black NGK and went to live in Mamelodi township near Pretoria. "If my children do

RAFS MAYET

not learn to become white Africans, I am destroying their future," he has said.

A number of organisations, ranging from churches to Idasa, run encounter and bridge-building sessions for groups of people.

NVA authority Gene Sharp notes: "While social disobedience, a method of social non-cooperation, consists of the refusal to obey various social customs, rules, regulations, practices and behaviour patterns, another method of social intervention consists of new ways of behaviour which may positively contribute to the establishment of new social patterns."

ABOVE
Students at a mission school in Natal boycott exams in 1989.

■ JUBILANT BLACKS WELCOME 1 000 WHITES

A WARM welcome from an estimated 10 000-strong black crowd met 1 000 white marchers to a South African black township yesterday.

More than 1 000 whites, including children and several senior citizens, marched behind clergymen to convey a message of "peace, goodwill and hope" to the residents of New Brighton township in Port Elizabeth.

The white marchers set out from Livingstone Hospital soon after 10.30am, accompanied by about 5 000 blacks.

They were met by a 2km line of waving, cheering blacks who shook the hands of passing marchers and fell in behind them.

31

March marshalls squeezed 10 000 people into New Brighton's Centenary Hall at 1pm for an exchange of messages from local black leaders, and a church service. The Rev Nkululeko Tunyiswa, a spokesman for the Interdenominational African Ministers' Association of SA, welcomed the marchers "not as friends or neighbours but as brothers or sisters".

"I hope this is not the end but the beginning – you can see for yourselves that you are more than welcome," he said.

A message from recently released ANC leader Mr Raymond Mhlaba called for the formation of one Port Elizabeth City Council.

– Sunday Star, 26.11.89

■ WHITES IN BLACK TOWNSHIPS 'A BREAK-THROUGH'

MAMELODI. – Outside toilets, cornmeal for dinner and police visits in the middle of the night gave 170 white Christians a taste of everyday life in this black township last week.

While soldiers checked cars entering the township a few hundred metres away, the black hosts and their white guests braaied boerewors and dipped white cornmeal from a huge iron pot while discussing the four-day encounter at a picnic on Saturday night.

The event, designed to bring whites and blacks together and break down apartheid barriers, was organised by two Christian groups and ended yesterday with everyone going to church together in the township and in nearby Pretoria.

Mr Murray Hofmeyr, 29, a white theology student, was asked repeatedly to tell how police had come to the door at 3.30am on Friday to arrest him and his host, black churchworker Mr Sandy Lebese. He said they refused to say why and "were very rude".

Police freed Mr Hofmeyr a few hours later "when I finally convinced them what was going on, that there were 170 white people staying in the township that night – they didn't believe me".

Mr Lebese, who was imprisoned from 1977 to 1983 on a sabotage conviction, was held in detention without explanation.

The delegates, including about 40 blacks who stayed in white homes in Pretoria, tried to adopt a joint statement at the end of their encounter that would reflect their mutual experience, but found that they could not.

"Apartheid was very successful," said the Rev Nico Smith, one of the principal organisers.

"It succeeded to divide the people, to separate them from one another. It eventually ended up with the whites fearing the blacks and the blacks being furious with the whites, and you know anger and fear is a recipe for violence."

Mr Smith promoted a separate message from the whites to tell other whites what they had learnt.

Mr David Ramakgadi, a church fieldworker, read the blacks' statement, which said: "We are thrilled that at last, after a struggle of more than 50 years, you have come to our township not to tell us, but to listen."

– Cape Times, 21.3.88

We are thrilled that at last, after a struggle of more than 50 years, you have come to our township not to tell us, but to listen.

CAMOUFLAGE

Camouflage may become necessary when meetings and other activities are restricted. Political meetings have been held under the auspices of organisations with totally different purposes such as sport, amusement, art or religion.

In 1904 in Russia, opponents of the Tsar used "banquets" as a disguise for strategic meetings.

Z K Mathews, Cape president of the ANC in the 1950s, records that at the 1954 conference of the Cape Congress:

"While a reception was being held at the (Uitenhage) location hall, the delegates were quietly removed to another place where, all night, the real business of the conference was discussed without members of the security branch being present." (*Freedom For My People*)

■ ACTIVISTS FIND A MOBILE SOLUTION TO EMERGENCY CLAMP ON MEETINGS

WHILE it hurtles across the industrial landscape of the East Rand at dusk, ferrying workers from factories to their homes in Tembisa, the 5pm train from Germiston becomes the vehicle for an ingenious response to the state of emergency.

Comrade Jabu – he asked for his real name not to be used because police have mounted raids on the train lines to Witwatersrand townships – told the *Weekly Mail* how union members and youth activists have, under emergency conditions, turned train coaches into effective platforms for trade union and township campaigns.

On the Germiston-Tembisa line, he says, support was won among commuters for striking metalworkers during the national strike last year; the rent boycott in Tembisa; the mass three-day protest in June last year against the new labour Bill; and a boycott of a fish and chip shop near Elandsfontein which sold rotten sausages to workers.

"Train committees" have been established to co-ordinate these campaigns. Another of their tasks has been to stop "thugs and tsotsis" from harassing people at stations. Jabu says this is a major reason for the blessing that commuters have given the committees.

"They trust us because we have cleaned up the stations," Jabu says. "But it is not always easy to keep their attention – especially if the

speeches are too long. If you speak from here to the next station you are in big trouble. So we sing and dance to keep them interested."

Comrade Jabu, sacked last year from the company in Elandsfontein where he had been an active shop steward, now describes himself as a "cultural worker" on the trains. "In 1987 I saw that interest in the train meetings was beginning to die down. So I decided to make a play to show on the trains. Most of our people like to sing and dance and act. If we entertain the people, they are more likely to support our struggle."

One of the plays devised and acted out in the coaches was called *Workers' Lament*. Another popular play on the 5pm train to Tembisa is called *Women Stand Up For Your Rights*.

"It shows the threefold exploitation that black women suffer as wives, workers and community members," says Jabu. "We wanted to persuade the men in the train to treat their women better."

Trade unionists report that similar happenings have become commonplace on Witwatersrand lines where large groups of workers commute to and from work. Shop stewards often arrange what is increasingly becoming the workers' answer to the businessman's breakfast: a quick meeting in the carriage to discuss strategy. In a recent edition of the *Labour Bulletin*, researcher Kehla Shubane argues that trains have become a major venue in which the political culture that developed in the townships during the 1984-1986 insurrection is being kept alive.

– Weekly Mail, 15.6.89

See also: Jogging and jolling, Underground

> **The meek inherit the earth because they are adaptable and learn fast.**
> **– Kenneth Boulding**

CAMPAIGN

Campaigns are usually launched as a method of protest and persuasion, aiming to mobilise people and opinions. More ambitious campaigns, like the mass defiance campaigns of 1952 and 1989, also encompass non-cooperation and intervention. Extra-parliamentary movements in SA campaign separately but also combine to act in concert on specific "single issues".

The ECC's month-long project of alternative service – Working For A Just Peace – mounted in April 1986, serves as a good example of a single organisation, single issue campaign.

Schoolchildren, students, young professionals, housewives and elderly people joined ECC activists in symbolic protest against conscription and in favour of alternative national service by working on projects seen as of genuine service to the nation.

Projects included planting wheat outside a military base (Durban), renovating a creche and old age home (PE), hosting picnics (Johannesburg and Durban), planting trees at Compensation resettlement camp (Pietermaritzburg) and cleaning up the polluted Liesbeek River (Cape Town).

The campaign built the image of ECC as a "positive" organisation, raised the issue of alternative service in the public eye, created a sense of community responsibility, actively involved individuals, and extended relations between ECC and a range of organisations and individuals.

See also: Anniversaries

CIVIL DISOBEDIENCE

Author Gene Sharp calls civil disobedience "one of the most drastic forms of political non-cooperation" and "an expression of the doctrine that there are times when men have a moral responsibility to disobey 'man-made' laws in obedience to 'higher' laws". "At least since Socrates," he says, "members of religious and political groups have experienced a conflict of loyalties.

"Modern justification is frequently based on a conviction that obedience would make one an accomplice to an immoral or unjust act or one which is seen to be, in the last analysis, itself illegal."

In the classical nonviolence tradition of both Gandhi and King, a campaign of civil disobedience is seen as a last resort. Their view was that it should be undertaken only after other methods of settling conflict have been exhausted, and under conditions favourable to a peaceful outcome.

The most important condition is that people should be trained and disciplined.

In March 1919, Gandhi was briefly arrested and news of this sparked riots and killings in several centres. Gandhi felt he had made "a Himalayan miscalculation" by unleashing a civil disobedience campaign without educating people on the "meaning and inner significance of satyagraha".

In 1921, Gandhi again suspended civil disobedience – to the initial bewilderment and indignation of some of his supporters – when a clash between protesters and police ended in the deaths of 22 policemen. (Kumar and Puri: *Mahatma Gandhi, His Life and Influence*, Heinemann, London, 1982)

In SA in July 1987, the SACC adopted a resolution which questioned the legitimacy of the government in the light of the heretical nature of apartheid, and recommended to member churches that they should question their moral obligation to obey laws like the Group Areas Act, the Education Acts and the Separate Amenities Act.

"Individual Christians have to consider the laws of the government and ask themselves whether these are the laws of God or the laws of a tyrant . . . and then respond accordingly, Prof Charles Villa-Vicencio said in an interview with *Crisis News*. "This could involve conscientious disobeying of certain laws by certain individuals."

The adoption of the Lusaka Statement at the same time caused disquiet among some members of the English-speaking churches. The statement noted that "while remaining committed to peaceful change we recognise that the nature of the SA regime, which wages war against its own inhabitants and neighbours, compels the liberation movements to the use of force along with other means to end oppression." *Crisis News*, produced by the WPCC, responded in May 1988 by drawing attention to three "nonviolent campaigns fully endorsed by the SACC and supported over the last few years" – the rent boycott, an alternative system of registration of births in defiance of the Population Registration Act, and a campaign upholding the principle of "no taxation without representation" (see *Withholding tax*).

The same issue of *Crisis News* quoted pacifist the Rev Rob Robertson: "I think there may be a current misunderstanding about civil disobedience. Every so often a leader in the liberation struggle is quoted as suggesting that civil disobedience has been made ineffective, difficult or even impossible by some new state enactment.

"A recent example is a group of theologians looking at the post-Kairos situation and saying: 'We are less confident about the viability of staging civil disobedience programmes than we were a year ago.' Someone even said: 'Civil disobedience has been made illegal', as if it wasn't always illegal.

"I worry that these sentiments are an unconscious way of allowing a wider range than ever for violence as the other option. Of course violence is also usually illegal (unless the state does it!) – as well as being of questionable morality."

In any nonviolent campaign there are four basic steps: collection of the facts, negotiation, self-purification and direct action. – *Martin Luther King*

■ 'WE WON'T OBEY' KAGISO IN HEAD-ON COLLISION WITH STATE

THE Kagiso Trust, SA's largest anti-apartheid fund, is set for a head-on collision with the government over the Foreign Funding Disclosure Act.

Since the government is certain to go ahead with its threat to force the trust to reveal information in terms of the Act, and the trustees are determined not to comply, a major showdown appears inevitable.

This will involve high-profile community and church leaders who serve as trustees, such as Archbishop Desmond Tutu; Frank Chikane, the current general secretary of the SACC, and his predecessor, Beyers Naudé; and the Human Rights Commission's Max Coleman, all of whom could face criminal charges if the trust does not comply.

It could also cause a major diplomatic incident, since the trust's major donor is the European Community which includes some of SA's biggest trading partners, such as Britain and West Germany.

These countries' large donations to the fund have formed a key part of their arguments against further sanctions against SA, as it has enabled them to argue that their role here is a positive one. Breaking the trust could fuel the sanctions campaign by making it more difficult for anti-sanctions governments to sustain this argument.

The trust this week made representations to the government after receiving a warning that it would be declared a "reporting" organisation in terms of the Act. This would force the trustees to disclose all its foreign funds, the names of donors, and the purpose for which the money was given.

However, it is almost certain the government will go ahead with its threatened move.

According to the executive director of the trust, Achmat Dangor, the trust has not changed its decision to defy any government attempt to force it to disclose details of its funds.

Lawyers said Kagiso was likely to be charged for non-compliance, and the accused – which could include any of its trustees – would face a maximum penalty of a R40 000 fine and three years imprisonment. The funds could be frozen during any such prosecution.

If the trust were found guilty, then the court could either send the funds back to the donor or, where the foreign donor could not be located, send it to the registrar of foreign funds, a post created by the Act.

The registrar would in turn channel the funds to the minister of finance who would decide how the money should be spent, bearing in mind the purpose for which it was given.

Trustee Beyers Naudé told *Weekly Mail:* "Kagiso Trust's main objection to the Act is the vast administrative powers the state acquires to gather intelligence about opponents of apartheid."

The trust has resolved:

● Not to obey those sections of the law which are blatantly of an intelligence-gathering nature and that could lead to the prosecution of others;

● To call on its biggest donor, the EC, and its member states, to voice their opposition to the Act;

● To call for strong punitive measures should the government threaten to disrupt the resources of those who engage in peaceful opposition to apartheid.

– Weekly Mail, 1.9.89

■ DEFIANCE AND THE RULE OF LAW

MORE than four decades of repression by successive National Party governments has depended heavily upon a single assumption – that black political dissidents can be rendered ineffectual by the flurry of a ministerial signature. Thus over the years thousands of blacks have been silenced by no more than the issuing of a banning or restriction order; scores of organisations have been removed from the arena of legitimate politics merely by a notice in the Government Gazette.

What the system of repression has depended on for its remarkable efficacy over the years has been the voluntary acquiescence of the victims.

What this system of repression has depended on for its remarkable efficacy over the years has been the voluntary acquiescence of the victims. Those banned or restricted have, by and large, obeyed the conditions of their banning or restriction orders and there have been comparatively few cases of disobedience. Likewise, proscribed organisations have generally vanished from view, though some have gone underground and others have survived in new mutations.

While such acquiescence was wrought in part by the intimidatory powers of the state, it depended also on a pervasive respect for the authority and essential respectability of the law to which political dissidents so often turned – and still turn – for relief from oppression.

Now, in more desperate political times, the intimidatory powers of the state have waned; the veneration of the law has diminished with the erosion of the rule of law. Inevitably that meek acquiescence of yesteryear has evaporated and SA is now witnessing an open, deliberate and organised campaign of defiance.

It presents a momentous challenge to the government, for any major attempt to restore the intimidatory powers of the state would at best be a palliative and would undoubtedly carry a heavy cost in terms of further sanctions, isolation, loss of confidence, disruption and black embitterment.

The wise alternative is to recognise that the era of negotiation has dawned –

negotiation in an atmosphere free of repression, with all the leaders of SA, and not just those who the government is prepared to allow through the sieves and filters of repression.

– Weekend Argus editorial, 19.8.89

■ AMCHAM GIVES SA BOSSES A GUIDE ON CIVIL DISOBEDIENCE

A CIVIL disobedience programme for business has been proposed by the American Chamber of Commerce to its 500 corporate members in SA.

The programme was drawn up by the Get Ahead Foundation, a non-profit black business promotion organisation headed by Soweto Civic Association chairman Dr Ntatho Motlana, at the request of Amcham's social justice committee.

It contains "areas of action" where "racist laws clearly interfere with the lives of black people" and suggests that bosses act together in specific areas.

Among the action suggested is refusing to register staff under the Population Registration Act; giving long-term contracts, pensions and other benefits to migrant workers; providing housing assistance to staff with or without administration board approval; providing alternative transport for workers; encouraging integration of schools; paying legal fees of people prosecuted for adopting these suggestions.

– City Press, 9.8.86

See also: Defiance, Gandhi, King

CLOTHES

Political dissent or protest may be expressed by wearing particular colours, badges or clothes. A related form of protest – states of undress – is thousands of years old. Jeremiah was one of several Old Testament prophets who tore his clothes and donned sackcloth and ashes as a sign of grief and protest. In SA, the women of Mogopa wore sackcloth at an anniversary commemoration of their forced removal.

In Denmark during World War II, when the Nazis ordered Jews to wear a yellow star, King Christian announced that he and his family would adopt it as a badge of honour and invited all citizens of Denmark to do likewise.

In SA, families of people on trial for involvement with the banned ANC sometimes attended court wearing clothes in the green, black and gold colours of the organisation.

On August 12, 1987, 13 young ANC members and sympathisers wore track-suits in those colours on the day they were sentenced to long terms in jail.

Many people wear T-shirts with political slogans and the Black Sash is named for the mourning band its members have worn on protest stands since 1955.

During the detainees' hunger strike of 1989, many people wore red ribbons to signify solidarity with the struggle of the detainees.

PROSECUTION SEES RED AT ANC'S COURT FASHION

BLACK, green and gold – the colours of the ANC – look set to become the hottest combination on the SA alternative fashion scene this summer.

Leading the way in the left-wing fashion stakes this week – much to the consternation of the state – were Broederstroom trialists Susan Westcott, Damian de Lange and Iain Robertson.

The Pretoria Regional Court, where the trial of the ANC military cell arrested in Broederstroom last year is being played out, has become the setting for a vivid display of support for the banned organisation.

On Wednesday, recently released ANC leaders Mr Walter Sisulu, Mr Ahmed Kathrada, Mr Elias Motsoaledi and Mr Andrew Mlangeni were in court to show their support for the trio.

To welcome their attendance, the trialists and many members of the public gallery wore colourful splashes of black, green and gold.

Westcott has worn striking combinations of the colours since the trial began in July. But on the day her co-trialists decided to follow her lead with their black, green and gold ties, the prosecution team decided to object.

The magistrate promptly ruled the colours a contravention of legislation concerning a banned organisation and ordered their removal.

– Sunday Times, 5.11.89

'A LESS PATIENT AGE'

THE T-shirt has become as much a point of group identification as it is a breathtakingly efficient way of communicating ideas. The hottest items on sale on Sunday (at the welcome home rally for released ANC leaders at Soccer City) were two different ANC-supporting T-shirts, one emblazoned "ANC Lives! ANC Leads!", the other with photographs of the recently released leaders.

According to an organiser of the event, one of the few misdemeanours to take place on Sunday involved the theft of a whole carton of these shirts – by youths whose desire to own one of these pieces of memorabilia overran their bank balances.

– Weekly Mail, 3.11.89

BLACK ARMBAND MOURNS NAT RULE

A BLACK armband worn in the Assembly by the Independent MP for Claremont, Mr Jan van Eck, should be ruled out of order according to Mr Kobus Bosman (NP Germiston Central).

Mr Bosman said yesterday Mr Van Eck had told him the armband was in mourning for 40 years of NP rule.

– The Argus, 27.5.88

Law and order are always and everywhere the law and order which protect the established hierarchy.
 – *Herbert Marcuse*

39

■ NAKED PROTEST

HANOVER. – About 200 men and women paraded naked through the centre of Hanover yesterday to protest against an exhibition of electronic weaponry.

A police spokesman said the demonstration was not considered offensive. "It made a pleasant change," he commented.

– The Argus, 20.5.82

CODES

Nonviolent action operates on the basis of a strict code of ethics (see *Civil disobedience*). The success of the Defiance Campaign of 1952 owed much to its code of discipline which volunteers pledged to respect. They agreed to remain nonviolent no matter what the provocation, to be erect, alert, clean, calm, sober and to submit willingly to arrest.

Similar principles guided nonviolent activists in the 1989 defiance campaign.

Guidelines for equal rights in the workplace, set out by the Rev Leon Sullivan in 1977, became the standard code of ethics for 196 US companies doing business in SA. Sullivan, who is pastor of the Zion Baptist Church in Philadelphia, announced additions to his code in May 1986, urging businesses into active challenge of all apartheid laws.

■ TACTICS FOR A DAY AT THE STRAND

DESMOND Tutu does not swim but he has pledged to paddle tomorrow in the surf at The Strand, a whites-only beach in the Western Cape.

A similar attempt last month was met with a beach cordoned off with candy-striped tape and signs warning "Danger: SAP dog-trainings". The defiant few who made it to the water's edge were later dispersed by police using dogs and sjamboks.

Careful planning has gone into tomorrow's fresh attempt. One of the objects is to have people moving on to the beach in a way that does not intimidate or threaten the locals – white, elderly and conservative.

In terms of guidelines drawn up for the protest, protesters will:
● Be open and respectful towards the people they encounter;
● Will not engage in physical violence or verbal abuse towards anyone;
● Will not destroy property and will clear up litter before leaving;
● Will not bring or use alcohol or drugs, except for medicinal purposes;
● Will carry no weapons;
● Will submit to the discipline of their leaders.

– Weekly Mail, 22.9.89

See also: Austerity, Programmes, Satyagraha, Wading in

CONSCIENTIOUS OBJECTION

The SA debate on conscientious objection began with a resolution adopted at an SACC conference in Hammanskraal in 1974. Noting the increasing militarisation of SA, the resolution asked "whether Christ's call to take up the cross and follow him in identifying with the oppressed does not, in our situation, involve becoming conscientious objectors?"

Some objectors are religious pacifists while others take their stand on secular political or moral grounds, with a range of other positions in between. Charles Bester, initially sentenced to six years imprisonment at the age of 18, objected on the grounds of his opposition to apartheid, although an essentially religious quality to his objection could clearly have earned him community service instead.

"The network of conscientious objector support groups which began developing from 1979, and the annual gatherings of these groups and other sympathisers in mid-year conferences – begun in 1980 – had always to deal with the tension between universal and selective objection," SB Brittion and PM Graham observe in "The Conflict of Conscription "(*Conscientious Objection,* Occasional Paper No 8, Centre for Intergroup Studies).

"The Defence Amendment Act of 1983 appeared to be especially written to foster these potential divisions. It provided for those who had universal religious objections to military service; it excluded any who appeared to have political reasons."

Brittion and Graham introduced the debate on conscription at a CIS workshop in 1983, and at the fourth objectors' conference the End Conscription Campaign was launched.

"It had the advantage of being a single-issue campaign, of being legal as opposed to the quasi-legality of the propagation of objection, of not being reliant on personal witness and martyrdom, and of being sustainable for those reasons. It enabled the building of alliances with organisations and individuals outside the sphere of conscientious objection, and it captured the moment when SA society was about to enter a period of unprece-

RIGHT
Conscientious objectors, led by CF Captain André Zaaiman (centre), gather in Cape Town in August 1988.

ERIC MILLER

dented militarisation and resistance," they note.

The ECC was restricted in its activities in 1985, restricted as an organisation in 1988, and in between suffered the harassment and detention of many of its leaders as well as a smear campaign conducted by the SADF.

By 1989 the objection debate had refocused on alternative national service and some theorists, including Brittion and Graham, were questioning the advantages of ending conscription – which can have a democratising and anti-polarising effect on society.

The core issue for most objectors remained service in a defence force deployed to maintain minority rule (see *Questioning)*. Groups of objectors have made public stands refusing to serve in the SADF since 1987.

One of the group of 143 who announced their objection in four cities in August 1988 was André Zaaiman, a CF captain who resigned his commission and refused to do reserve duty. At a subsequent forum on conscription he said: "Objection is an act of value definition, of setting unambiguous parameters for your morality. In objecting one rejects certain things; in this case the right of an illegitimate state to conscript you and consequently force you to defend a system that is indefensible."

■ SAYING NO

CONSCIENTIOUS objection is an attempt to bring back the dimension of moral choice, says Andries du Toit, one of the 771 men who recently refused to serve in the SADF.

He was one of the original group of 23 who made their refusal to serve public in August 1987. Today he admits that he wasn't ready then to deal with the consequences of his decision.

(As a student he has been able to get deferment but when he completes his Masters degree he will be liable for call-up and could face six years in jail.)

"Before I made my choice, I couldn't think about the future. I lived from year to year. Since my decision I have hope. Now I can drive past little Karoo towns like Merweville and know that I'll still be here in 40 years time," he says.

During a year in the US at the age of 16 he "experienced intense debates on moral issues. I realised then that one can make choices. It may sound dramatic, but I went to the US opposed to apartheid and came back identifying with the struggle."

– Democracy in Action, October 1989

■ 6 YEARS' JAIL FOR ARMY OBJECTOR

JOHANNESBURG. – Members of a packed Johannesburg Magistrate's Court wept yesterday as former Wits student David Bruce was given the maximum six years' sentence for refusing to serve in the Defence Force.

Bruce, 25, who pleaded not guilty last Tuesday, said he refused to serve in an army that upheld a racist government.

He is the first South African to have refused to do any military service and stayed in the country to face the consequences.

In mitigation of sentence yesterday, Soweto Civic Association president Dr Ntatho Motlana said Bruce would be regarded as a hero in the black community

Military intelligence is a contradiction in terms.
– Groucho Marx

for his principled stand against racism.

During the well-attended trial last week David's blind mother, Mrs Ursula Bruce, gave evidence in mitigation. She recalled her experiences as a Jew growing up in Nazi Germany before she and her family fled to SA in 1939.

"Of my very closest family 12 died in the Holocaust," Mrs Bruce said. "I still have a deep sense of gratitude and obligation to SA, but I cannot avoid being very, very aware of certain points of similarity."

- Cape Times, 26.7.88

■ BRUCE was the first person to be tried under the 1983 amendment to the Defence Act which makes provision for religious objectors to do alternative community service, but steps up the penalties for non-religious objectors.

Two people previously convicted under the Act were convicted for not reporting to camps. Philip Wilkinson received a R600 fine in 1987 and Ivan Toms a 630-day sentence in March 1988.

Before the Defence Act was amended, 12 people went to jail or detention barracks for periods of up to two years for refusing to do military service on moral or religious grounds.

– Weekly Mail, 29.7.88

COURT ACTION

When governments pass legislation that erodes or destroys the rule of law, as is the case in SA, the protective function of the courts is weakened or lost. An additional flaw in the system, partially addressed by institutions like state-subsidised legal aid and privately funded legal resources centres, is that the protection of the courts is often beyond the financial resources of most citizens.

Despite this, and notwithstanding the fact that NVA in South Africa has included defiance and civil disobedience, anti-apartheid organisations have made the use of legal means – ranging from on-the-spot lawyers to negotiate with police at meetings and marches, to formal court action – a powerful weapon. In so doing, they have upheld and strengthened the ideal of the rule of law.

■ KILOMETRE OF PAPERWORK FOR X-ROADS CLAIMS

THE amount of work which went into processing 3 300 damages claims against the SA police, arising from the Crossroads conflict, became apparent yesterday as field workers spoke of long days in the field, a kilometre of computer paperwork and stories of personal loss.

A squatter refugee cried as she asked if she could claim for her pet tortoise. Another told of fighting in vain to save her dying child from the flames of their shack.

And the researchers believe a crucial precedent has been set – for the first time impoverished people in the black communities have discovered on a mass basis that they too are entitled to seek help from the courts.

Most claims are for simple household goods – primus stoves, children's clothing, furniture, zinc and plastic sheeting. The total amount being claimed from the Minister of Law and Order is R4 812 781.

– Cape Times, 13.11.86

See also: Affidavit, Alternative structures

COURTING ARREST

Requests for arrest are often made to show solidarity with people already arrested, but may also demonstrate the absence of fear of arrest – in other words, the failure of coercion on the opponent's part. Where many people are involved, the aim may be to clog the courts and fill the prisons (see *Overloading*).

■ FILM OF PROTESTERS SHOWN IN COURT

A PAARL magistrate was yesterday shown a police video film of Mbekweni rent protesters demanding to be taken to the Paarl police station and climbing freely into a waiting police vehicle, singing and laughing.

After one group had been taken to the Paarl police station, a second group had demanded the same treatment.

– Cape Times, 6.10.83

See also: Defiance

DEFIANCE

The most famous example in SA history of this mass method of civil disobedience is the Defiance of Unjust Laws Campaign of 1952. It may, however, yield pride of place to the defiance campaign of 1989.

A remarkable aspect of the 1989 campaign was that many of the organisations and people taking part "unbanned" themselves in order to do so. And not only did the 1989 campaign, unlike that of 1952, take-place against the background of a state of emergency – it effectively ended it.

The campaign included a wide range of actions, some of which are reflected under specific entries (see *Marches, Wading in).*

■ DEFINING DEFIANCE

What did the Defiance Campaign set out to achieve?

We aimed to make apartheid laws unworkable. We targeted four main areas. Firstly, the state of emergency really hampered the MDM. It was being used to prevent us from organising and to restrict hunger strikers who were released from detention. We had lived for too long with these curbs on our activities – defying restrictions on organisations and individuals was a key part of the campaign.

Petty apartheid was our second target. We wanted to have masses of people showing up the farce of separate hospitals and beaches.

A third area has been the Labour Relations Amendment Act. The LRA is seen by the MDM as a clear attack on workers. Given the central role which Cosatu, and workers generally, are playing in the MDM, it was felt we needed to target that aspect of apartheid legislation as part of the Defiance Campaign.

Fourthly, the campaign was aimed at the whole tricameral system. The effective boycott of the coloured and Indian Houses was an indication of the unworkability of the tricameral system.

Besides making these laws unworkable, we also needed to rebuild our own structures. Our organisations were demoralised and our communication was not good. We needed an injection of life and energy.

We also wanted to bring back the sense of mass participation which we saw in 1985 and 1986. After three years of a state of emergency, ordinary people have been filled with lethargy and fear. We needed to break that down.

Finally, we aimed to send a very clear message to the international community. We wanted to say that the MDM is a powerful force in this country. Any solution to SA's problems must take our organisations seriously.

Could you comment on the major gains that have been achieved by the campaign?

The Defiance Campaign has shown people that the mass movement is real and visible. We have been popular and attractive in projecting our demands and uniting people around our vision.

We've succeeded, in many ways, in rendering the state of emergency unworkable. It's still on the statute books but the fact that normal municipal regulations or the Internal Security Act have been used to deal with the legal applications for recent marches, rather than using the emergency regulations, shows our success.

The fear which has developed over the last few years due to the intense repression has been largely overcome by the activities of the Defiance Campaign.

Compared to 1985, the mobilisation is a lot more mature. Because it's directed at winnable demands, it has popular support.

Now we hope to see the transformation of support into strong and solid organisations. The alliance between the UDF and Cosatu has been strengthened. We have demonstrated very clearly to the government that the MDM is a very powerful mass force that cannot be ignored.

Also, for the first time, there were people participating whom one had never seen at such activities before – the mayor of Cape Town, business executives, DP leadership and many many others. Whites are beginning to identify with the vision projected by the MDM. This is very significant for the resolution of SA's conflict.

The fact that there are now nearly 780 objectors as opposed to 143 last year (and many more who share the same sentiment) is an indicator of how whites are responding.

Do you think FW has succeeded in getting the credit for allowing certain marches to go ahead?

The march would have gone ahead whether FW allowed it or not. The fact that he granted permission for it was a result of the success of our Defiance Campaign. The lack of police interference proved that violence does not stem from protesters but from police. It is a great victory that the marches went off peacefully.

Are there plans for the Defiance Campaign to continue? Is there a cut-off point?

The Defiance Campaign will continue . . . as long as apartheid laws exist, the Defiance Campaign will be there.

– Interview with Cameron Dugmore, *Upfront, November 1989*

Compared to 1985, the mobilisation is a lot more mature. Because it's directed at winnable demands, it has popular support.

WHITE HOSPITALS WILL NEVER BE THE SAME

BEFORE this week, a visit to the hospital for Patricia Khumalo of kwaMashu would take the whole day.

She would leave her home in the Natal township at 5am for King Edward Hospital, stand in interminable queues before being treated, and get home, exhausted, late in the afternoon.

On Wednesday she rose just before 8am, and barely two hours later was being treated at the whites-only Addington Hospital.

It was a pleasant change: so much so that she has no intention of going back to the much less convenient King Edward. As a result of her participation in the MDM's campaign of defiance against segregated facilities, Khumalo has decided to get her medical care where it's closest and quickest.

"I'll demand to be treated here," she said. "I think I have a right, as a South African, to use any hospital."

Hers was one of many hundreds of such acts of defiance by black patients in the Transvaal and Natal on the first day of the MDM campaign, and it symbolises a blow to one of apartheid's softest spots – the discriminatory provision of medical care.

MDM leaders say white hospitals will never be the same after this week's action; that the enforced bending of the law has established a principle for the future.

The peaceful and orderly protest at eight hospitals in the two provinces was certainly a major propaganda success for the MDM.

It passed off peacefully despite doomsday predictions by Minister of Law and Order Adriaan Vlok about "incitement to violence".

– Weekly Mail, 4.8.89

MINERS ADD MUSCLE TO DEFIANCE MOVES

BLACK mineworkers around the country have added their muscle to the defiance campaign launched by resistance groups this week.

The 200 000-strong National Union of Mineworkers (NUM) yesterday announced its members had staged protests in segregated toilets, canteens, change rooms and mine medical stations around the country.

NUM said the protests included:

● A lunchtime sit-in at the all-white canteen of Mintek research laboratory by about 200 workers yesterday.

● At the Ergo Refinery in Brakpan black workers yesterday began using change rooms for white miners.

● Management of the Impala Platinum Refinery in Springs locked its all-white toilets and issued keys to white workers after black labourers defied segregation in the latrines.

● Since Monday black workers from Anglo American's Springfield Colliery have been riding on white buses and white workers have refused to board with them.

● A shaft steward at the Lyttelton Dolomite Mine in Pretoria has been charged for making tea in a kitchen reserved for whites.

● On July 20 black workers used change rooms for whites-only on Anglo American's President Steyn Gold Mine in the Free State.

● On July 30 police prevented Rustenburg mineworkers from staging a sit-in at parks reserved for whites.

– Weekly Mail, 4.8.89

■ PRICE OF A DEFIER'S BUS FARE – CHARGES OF CONSPIRACY

"I HATE the white buses. It took me two days to reach my workplace on the white buses. They're horrible." This was the conclusion reached by the Rev Gideon Makhanya, one of this week's Pretoria "bus apartheid" defiers.

But, like the buses or not, Makhanya paid a price for trying them out. Makhanya, who has been released on bail, was one of 13 people – fieldworkers of the Pretoria Council of Churches and Koinonia, as well as students – arrested after attempting to board whites-only buses in the capital.

Some have been charged with "conspiracy", and others with conspiracy and contravention of the Separate Amenities Act.

The bus action formed part of one of the nationwide defiance campaign's most innovative initiatives: turning the time-honoured bus boycott tactic on its head, blacks demanding access to white buses with the aim of having them eventually desegregated.

Most were unsuccessful, but the point was made dramatically. This week, in response to groups of black people gathering at bus stops, municipal buses went empty, leaving white commuters puzzled, stranded – and late for work.

– Weekly Mail, 1.9.89

■ A SATURDAY OF A KIND SECUNDA HADN'T SEEN

THE Conservative Party stronghold of Secunda has been put on the political map – by 5 000 toyi-toying workers brandishing an "Unban the ANC" banner.

The little Eastern Transvaal dorp, dominated by the Sasol II plant, has never attracted much opposition attention. However, last Saturday, almost 5 000 workers marched to the local police station and presented a petition protesting the "anti-union Labour Relations Act".

They were part of more than 100 000 workers round the country who marched against the labour legislation in response to a call from Cosatu and the National Council of Trade Unions.

Moments before the start of the march police informed union officials "they did not have permission to march". But nothing could persuade the crowd they needed permission.

As a compromise, union officials negotiated for the marchers to take a short route to the police station – rather than walking right around the town.

– Weekly Mail, 20.10.89

ST GEORGE'S MEETING: UDF, OTHERS 'UNBANNED'

THE UDF and other restricted organisations "unbanned" themselves yesterday and a restricted activist spoke at a meeting in defiance of his restrictions as part of the MDM's defiance campaign.

Members of the UDF, NECC, Cayco, Western Cape Civic Association, Western Cape Students' Congress, Detainees Parents Support Committee and the ECC took part in a symbolic march yesterday to emphasise their "unbanning".

The march started at the Bell Tower of St George's Cathedral and stopped at the church hall before the procession returned to the cathedral.

Restricted UDF activists Mrs Hilda Ndude, Mr Willie Hofmeyr and Mr Roseberry Sonto and Cape Democrats leader Ms Amy Thornton walked under the UDF banner as marshalls, standing on either side of the procession.

They were among the group of 21 restricted people in the Western Cape at yesterday's service of witness, called by Archbishop Desmond Tutu after police banned a "people's rally" from being held at UWC.

Hundreds of people packed the cathedral and the church hall while the overflow packed the parking lot, listening to loudspeakers relaying speeches.

Restricted UDF leader Mr Trevor Manuel spoke as well as UDF national executive officer Murphy Morobe.

Several buses on their way to the service were stopped and turned away at a police roadblock erected on Settler's Way.

– The Argus, 21.8.89

RIGHT
Archbishop Desmond Tutu and others defy police in a march in Cape Town in August 1989.

ERIC MILLER

A three-stage plan of action was drawn up for the 1952 Defiance Campaign: (1) Acts of civil disobedience by "selected and trained persons" in major cities. (2) Increase in the number of such volunteers and in the number of cities in which to conduct acts of defiance. (3) Mass action "on a country-wide scale" involving people in both urban and rural areas.

Before the campaign a series of mass rallies were held in Cape Town, PE, East London, Pretoria and elsewhere, drawing as many as 10 000 people. Letters were sent to the government announcing plans for the campaign.

The government response was to threaten "full use of the machinery at its disposal" to deal with those "initiating subversive activities of any nature whatsoever".

On June 26 the campaign was launched, focusing on the ubiquitous sign "Europeans Only".

In the words of former ANC president and Nobel Peace Prize winner Chief Albert Luthuli: "Railway stations, waiting rooms, post offices, public seats, train accommodations, all bear this legend. The volunteers were to abandon the 'separate but unequal' facilities set aside for us, and to make challenging use of the alternative white facilities. In addition to this, the flouting of curfew and pass regulations was determined upon . . . . Whenever possible, the authorities were forewarned of the detailed intentions of each batch of volunteers – in some cases full lists of the names of volunteers were politely handed in."

The campaign gathered momentum and the discipline of the volunteers was excellent, according to Luthuli: so much so that on some occasions they took charge of traffic and crowd control when the authorities were unable to maintain order. Almost without exception those arrested – over 8 000 in all – chose to go to prison rather than pay a fine. The PE jail was more than once filled to capacity.

Coverage of the campaign by the white press was almost non-existent until people began to demonstrate outside court buildings and elsewhere. In August, for instance, *Press Digest* reported that 5 000 people held a prayer gathering in PE to welcome 250 volunteers on their release from prison.

At the height of the campaign, on October 18, a series of riots broke out in PE, Kimberley and East London. Several people – including a white nun – were killed, and buildings destroyed.

The ANC demanded a commission of inquiry but the government refused. Many people believed the riots were the work of agents provocateurs.

Luthuli's opinion was that the Defiance Campaign was too orderly and successful for the government's liking, and that it was growing. The prospect before the white supremacists, if they were going to react to the challenge in a civilised way, was that arrests would continue indefinitely.

He said that the challenge of nonviolence was more than the government could meet, because behind the thousands arrested, there were more, many more. Nonviolence on this scale robbed the authorities of the initiative. On the other hand, he understood that violence by Africans would restore that initiative to them – they would then be able to bring out the guns and the other techniques of

There are not enough jails, not enough policemen, not enough courts to enforce a law not supported by the people.
– Hubert Humphrey

initmidation and present themselves as restorers of order.

Other factors that caused the collapse of the campaign were the jailing of top leaders, new laws which gave the government sweeping powers to suppress and punish any defiance, and the breaking of discipline by ANC president-general Dr James Moroka.

He chose to be defended by his own lawyer (instead of jointly with the other 19 co-defendants in his case), and pleaded mitigating circumstances instead of being prepared to accept the full penalty of the law.

The campaign was officially ended a year after it began.

(Leo Kuper: *Passive Resistance in South Africa*, Yale University Press, 1957)

See also: Civil disobedience, Marches, Wading in

DEVIATING

Flouting or disregarding social customs and rules constitutes social intervention, particularly in an artificially divided society. It can also be a psychological tactic and a way of beginning new social patterns. Gandhi deviated from established practice by refusing to change his simple lifestyle or dress when he attended a round-table conference in London in 1931 as the sole delegate of the Indian National Congress.

When asked by someone why he chose to wear a loincloth only, he replied: "You wear plus fours, mine are minus fours."

Gandhi wore his "minus fours" to tea at Buckingham Palace. A reporter incensed by his failure to dress up for royalty asked Gandhi if he thought he had enough on.

Gandhi replied with a smile: "The king was wearing enough for both of us."

■ UNIONS WAGE PSYCHOLOGICAL WAR

WHEN it comes to negotiations between unions and employers, it's not only the physical forces both sides can muster that come into play – there are also the psychological aspects.

Both sides employ them, but it seems that union negotiators might be somewhat more inventive and adventurous in their tactics – especially given the cross-cultural elements that exist.

Unsettling the opposition is a move one organiser got quite gleeful about when describing employer reaction.

"Reactions vary, but some of them are totally baffled. They'll bring us tea. Instead of picking up the cup I leave it on the table and start slurping away," he said.

"They never know how to react. They just don't know what they've got on their hands."

– The Argus, 16.1.88

EARTHWRITING

This method of protest may not be particularly persuasive but deserves mention on the grounds of originality. It was used by a farmer in San Diego, California, after protests to a local US Air Force base about sonic booms had been ignored. In huge letters in a pasture he ploughed the word "QUIET" into the ground.

In December 1987, students at Wits University expressed their feelings about a circling police helicopter by using chairs to form a four-letter word big enough to be read from the air. A photograph of their work subsequently appeared in the *Weekly Mail*.

EXPOSÉ

Exposing injustice or maladministration, a specialised form of protest, becomes especially important – and difficult – where censorship helps those responsible to maintain an appearance of moral acceptability and social benefit.

The "official version" can be challenged through the formal media (see *Publishing*) or through letters, posters, pamphlets and cultural action. It can also be done by recourse to the courts.

◼ RIOT SQUAD CRITICISED BY SAP OFFICER

A POLICE lieutenant has described the action of members of the riot squad in his area as unprofessional and oppressive.

Lieutenant Gregory Rockman of Mitchells Plain police station said this as he described how he attempted to intervene when members of the squad broke up a placard demonstration by pupils in Mitchells Plain yesterday.

He said a major in the riot squad threatened to lock him up under the emergency regulations when he tried to stop the beatings and that afterwards he was summoned to the office of the Western Cape commissioner of police, Major-General Phillipus Fourie.

Lieutenant Rockman said that after scattering the "peaceful" demonstrators the riot squad used "excessive force" and injured an eight-month-pregnant woman.

Lieutenant Rockman, 30, crime prevention officer at Mitchells Plain, said he had been a lieutenant for three years and a policeman for 12.

"At this point in time I feel ashamed," he said. He said he was speaking out regardless of the consequences because this was a turning point in his life.

Lieutenant Rockman, whose work involves liaison with the community to prevent crime and eliminate points of friction, said he and colleagues had spoken at several schools during the unrest. "They (staff and students) listened to us but it's always a deadlock because the riot unit don't believe in dialogue."

– The Argus, 7.9.89

(Two riot squad policemen were subsequently charged with assault but acquitted on the basis that they were protected by the emergency regulations and for lack of evidence that they personally had committed assault. However, the magistrate noted that the beating of the Mitchells Plain demonstrators had been not only unlawful but "utterly reprehensible".)

RIGHT
Lieutenant Gregory Rockman at a press conference in Cape Town after criticising the police force for their behaviour in the townships.

Courtesy of THE ARGUS

■ 'I WOULD DO THE SAME AGAIN,' SAYS THE SPY WHO EXPOSED RENAMO

THE SADF intelligence corporal who first exposed the army's active support for Renamo emerged from nearly six years behind bars on Tuesday saying he had no regrets and was "completely unrehabilitated".

"If such a situation arose again I would do the same thing – only I'd do it better. I wouldn't get caught," said Roland Hunter a day after walking out of Pretoria Central.

Had it not been for the government's sensitivity about information Hunter passed on to ANC members Derek and Trish Hanekom, all three would be in prison for at least the next decade.

Instead the Hanekoms, who served shorter sentences, are now public ANC members based in Harare while Hunter is free to follow a career as an economist.

"I was gearing myself up for a 20-year sentence," said the tall 31-year-old. "But then they dropped the treason charges and I got the five-year maximum under the Defence Act for passing on military secrets to unauthorised persons."

The apparent reason for the lesser charges was the state's fear of the disclosure of the evidence Hunter had collected about the SADF's role in supporting Renamo – especially since there was talk of subpoenaing the state president.

Top cabinet officials met with the trio's advocate, the late Ernie Wentzel SC, and it was agreed that the trial would be held in camera and the three would plead guilty to lesser charges – Hunter under the Defence Act and the Hanekoms for possessing literature of a banned organisation.

For the rest of the world the story broke almost as soon as the three were charged. But at home the first legal suggestion of what happened came during a heated parliamentary debate in May 1985 when Graham McIntosh of the PFP accused the SADF of being "a major aggressor in Southern Africa".

– Weekly Mail, 29.9.89

■ DR WENDY ORR SPEAKS OUT ON TORTURE

ON September 25 1985, district surgeon Dr Wendy Orr hit world headlines when the PE Supreme Court granted her urgent application for an order restraining police from assaulting emergency detainees held in St Albans and North End prisons.

Dr Orr told the court that detainees complained "on a vast scale" of "brutal assaults" and they had injuries consistent with their claims.

The assaults were taking place during police interrogation, she said.

Because police were acting under the emergency regulations, and apparently believed they had been granted an immunity, some were "quite unrestrained" in the abuses they inflicted on detainees.

The Department of Prisons, it seemed to her, had "turned a blind eye". Complaints of assaults were not being investigated, Dr Orr said.

"Medical ethics and my conscience told me I had to do something," Dr Orr said. She also felt the detainees were "not in a position to do anything for themselves".

The Minister of Law and Order later agreed to pay the cost of the application – R259 819 – the only issue left to decide after the need for a final court order fell away when the emergency was – briefly – lifted.

After the court case, Dr Orr was barred from visiting detainees and confined to work in an old age home.

Supporters then paid off her State bursary – which required her to work for the government for three years – and she joined the Alexandra Health Clinic.

She also works for the detainees' support service of the National Medical and Dental Association. *The Star, 10.1.87; EP Herald; The Argus.*

See also: Affidavit, Court action

FLAGS

Displaying the flag or colours of a national, religious, social or political group is a common form of NV protest. Such displays often arouse deep emotion. In SA, the green, black and gold ANC flag is a powerful symbol for many people and was displayed at occasions like political funerals, in defiance of government bans. When mass marches and rallies were permitted in September 1989, both ANC and communist flags were freely unfurled.

■ THE RALLY WAS ANC, BUT THE DAY BELONGED TO THE RED FLAG

IF the crowd at Sunday's rally was the SA electorate and their roars votes, then Joe Slovo, other leaders of the SACP and Fidel Castro would now be planning the decor for their offices at the Union Buildings.

The SACP's message that democracy would create the conditions for the working class to push for socialism is clearly the favoured position of the militant township youth.

The claim by ANC president Oliver Tambo that it was in FW de Klerk's hands to become one of the peacemakers in SA was met with silence; the SACP's call to turn De Klerk's "tactical retreat" into "headlong flight" was cheered with gusto.

The big red flag of the SACP shared pride of place behind the rostrum with the black, green and gold banner of the ANC, but in the stands the SACP flags outnumbered those with the ANC colours.

– Weekly Mail, 3.11.89

■ UWC STUDENTS BURN FLAG AFTER CAMPUS MARCH

CLOSE to 1 000 students raised their fists in salutes and shouted "amandla ngawethu" (power to the people) as they watched flames leap from a burning SA flag at UWC yesterday.

As the flag disintegrated another flag bearing the green, black and gold colours of the banned ANC was raised.

The "new" flag was hoisted against a background of banners and posters displayed on the stage, spelling out the demands listed in the Freedom Charter. The students rallied in the main hall yesterday after marching around the campus buildings, singing and displaying posters protesting against the Republic Day celebrations.

– Cape Times, 28.5.81

If you want a symbolic gesture, don't burn the flag, wash it. – Norman Thomas

FRATERNISING

Personal contact with opponents can convince them that resistance is not aimed at them as individuals, and that the aims of the government they serve are unjust, Gene Sharp says in *The Methods of Nonviolent Action,* where this story about a campaign mounted in Czechoslovakia in 1968 appears:

"The following is an extract from a report in *Rude Pravo* by a Czech journalist, who had a 'lively discussion' with a Soviet captain, a Soviet lieutenant-colonel, two Soviet ambulance attendants, a Czech citizen and Czech ambulance attendants during the early stages of the Soviet invasion and occupation of Czechoslovakia in 1968:

"We presented our arguments about the invasion and when we parted we said: We shall not say au revoir, we shall not wish you luck and we shall not shake your hands.

"This was perhaps the ultimate argument. I actually saw tears in the eyes of the Soviet captain. The soldiers who had earlier just listened stood about hanging their heads.

"As we were leaving, the captain followed us a few steps and said: 'We shall all reflect about what we discussed here. I am afraid you are right about a number of things. It is a terrible tragedy and you can print that if you want to.' Within four days it proved necessary to rotate invasion troops and bring in replacements."

RIGHT
The ANC flag is wrapped around Louis Botha's statue in Adderley Street, Cape Town, during a protest rally in September 1989.

BENNY GOOL

FUNERALS

Mourning is a time-honoured method of protest and persuasion, and funerals of victims of state violence became powerful occasions for the expression of protest and solidarity in SA. At the height of repression and revolt in 1985 and 1986, tens of thousands of people attended political funerals.

The state reacted by imposing stringent curbs, such as limiting attendance numbers, requiring that only ministers of religion should speak, forbidding posters, banners, processions on foot, etc. A strong security force presence became a feature of most such funerals – as did defiance of restrictions.

Mourning is also observed beyond funerals. After the Sharpeville shootings of March 21 1960, both the ANC and the PAC called for a stayaway on March 28 in mourning for the 69 victims of the massacre.

■ SCENES OF ANGUISH AT FUNERALS OF VICTIMS

THOUSANDS of mourners gathered in Khayelitsha, Bellville and Lotus River yesterday to bury the victims of election night violence.

The funeral scenes served as a stark and tragic reminder of what had gone before Mr FW de Klerk's big peace gamble in allowing Wednesday's mass protest march in Cape Town which has set off similar marches in other centres without incident.

More than 800 people attended the service for 13-year-old Patrick Miller at the NG Sendingkerk in Bellville South.

Several banners were displayed inside the church, including those of the Bellville Students Congress and Cayco. Many of the mourners wore black, green and gold pennants – the colours of the ANC.

Dr Allan Boesak told mourners the tragedy should never have happened …

The anguished sobs of the family could be heard when the first hymn was sung at the graveside, and several minutes later Patrick's distraught sister Shirley had to be carried away.

A priest who spoke at the graveside said there was mourning all over the Western Cape because of unrest-related deaths. He said apartheid had to come to an end. If it did not, people would be standing at many more graves like this one. The funerals took place without police restriction.

– Sunday Star, 17.9.89

■ TEARGAS FIRED AT STUDENT'S FUNERAL

CAPE Town student leader Ashley Kriel was buried yesterday at a funeral at which police fired teargas.

Kriel, 20, was shot in controversial circumstances in Athlone last week. Police say he shot himself in a scuffle when they came to arrest him.

Yesterday's funeral service in the Cape Town suburb of Bonteheuwel was attended by more than 2 000 mourners, according to witnesses – in spite of police restrictions that only 800 could attend.

Mourners also defied other restrictions imposed by police in a special notice in the Government Gazette on Thursday.

Posters bearing Kriel's picture were placed on church walls, witnesses said, in spite of a police ban. A restriction that only ordained ministers could address the congregation was also ignored.

The defiance of the restrictions came after the refusal of a last-minute plea to police by church leader Dr Alan Boesak.

Negotiations between police and Dr Boesak – as well as PFP MP Mr Jan van Eck – continued while police surrounded the Bonteheuwel church at which the main service was held.

A spokesman for the police public relations division in Pretoria said no arrests were made at the funeral. He was not aware of the holding of any press photographers, although mourners said they saw several placed in a police van.

"There were a few minor incidents and a bit of tearsmoke was fired to disperse the crowd," the spokesman said.

– Sunday Tribune, 19.7.87

See also: Intervention

BELOW

The police try to remove the ANC flag from the coffin at the funeral of ANC cadre Ashley Kriel in 1987.

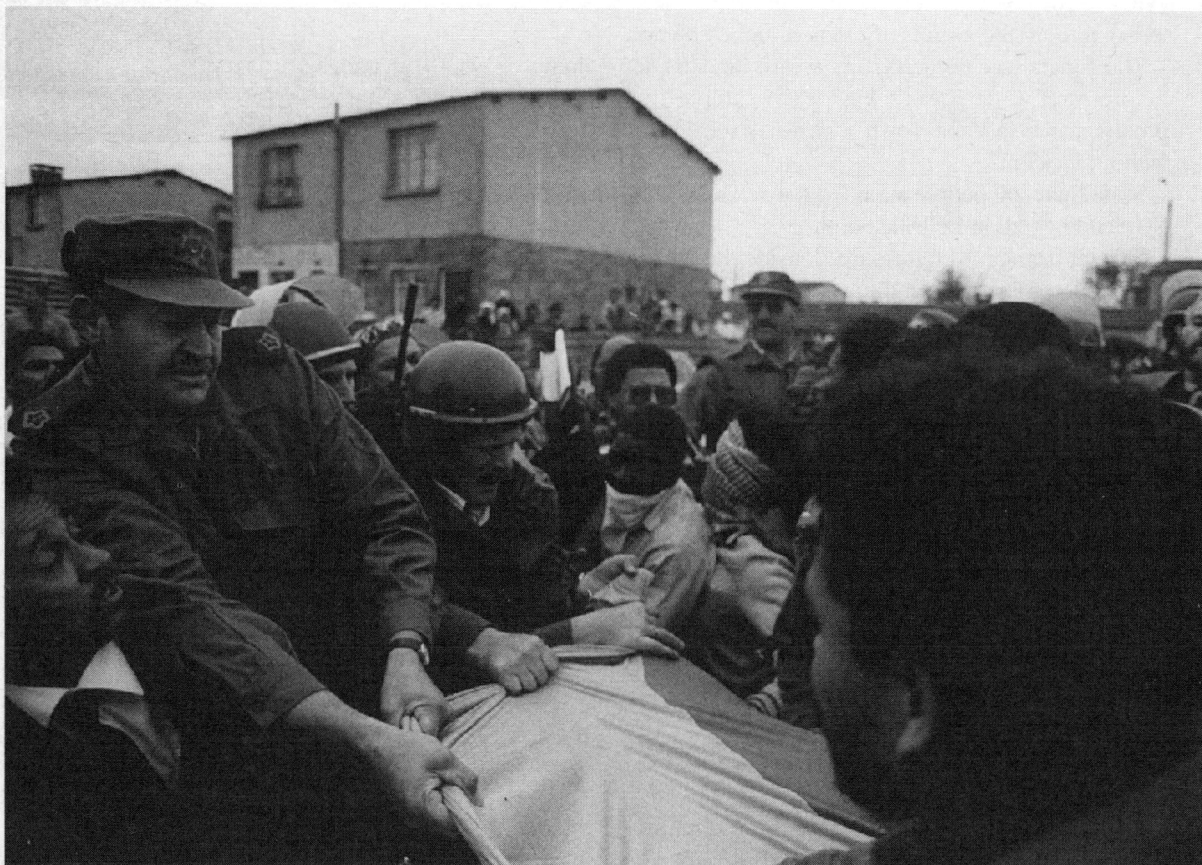

ROGER MEINTJES

GANDHI

Mohandas Karamchand Gandhi was given the title Mahatma – Great Soul – by India and by most of the world. He is remembered as a saintly leader, known for his advocacy of nonviolent resistance which was successful in ending British rule in India.

He was born in Porbandar, India, in 1869, but it was in South Africa that he began to evolve his method, which he called satyagraha and translated as "soul force" or "truth force". Central to this doctrine was his adamance that "truth may not be sacrificed for anything whatsoever".

Author James North describes the experience in SA that set Gandhi on his epic path.

"In the fall of 1893, a young lawyer named Mohandas K Gandhi disembarked in the port city of Durban. He was wearing a black turban, a starched white shirt, a black tie, a black frock coat, striped trousers, and glistening black patent leather shoes. He was 23 and he had studied law for three years in England. Two leading Indian merchants in SA had retained him to mediate a major financial dispute. He intended to remain in the country for one year. He observed the Hindu prohibition against eating meat, but otherwise he was not a social or political activist of any kind.

"A week after Gandhi arrived, he boarded a night train to Pretoria, 350 miles away, where one of the quarreling merchants lived. The dapper young lawyer naturally travelled first class. A white passenger demanded that he move back to the non-white car. Gandhi refused, and produced his first-class ticket. His appeal was ignored. A policeman ejected him from the train at Maritzburg. He spent the entire night shivering in the station, too embarrassed to ask for his baggage, which contained warmer clothing. In his autobiography, he described the long cold night as a turning point in his life. He wrote: 'The hardship to which I was subjected was superficial – only a symptom of the deep disease of colour prejudice. I should try, if possible, to root out the disease and suffer hardships in the process.'

"After further indignities en route, Gandhi arrived in Pretoria, where he promptly called the city's Indians to a series of meetings to discuss ways to fight racial discrimination. Thus began his extraordinary career.

RIGHT
Mahatma Gandhi, father of 20th century non-violent action.

He remained in SA for 20 years, during which he led huge cross-country protest marches, founded a newspaper, and established an experimental farm. He developed, step by step, his social and political philosophy. He gradually shed the garments in which he had arrived, and became the Gandhi recognised by history, clad in a simple white cloth dhoti and sandals. By the time he returned to India in 1914, he had established in SA an already strong tradition of nonviolent protest, a movement that would win an increasing number of adherents both within and outside the Indian community in the half-century to come." (*Freedom Rising*, Macmillan Publishing Company, 1985)

In his own words, Gandhi was both "an average man" and "a practical idealist". Yet over 400 books have been written about him, and his own collected works run to 85 volumes.

It is obviously impossible to do justice to such an accumulation of wisdom in a limited space. But if one initiative were to be singled out to illustrate Gandhi's peculiar genius, it must be the Salt March of 1930.

The British authorities treated it as a joke at first. They thought Gandhi was losing contact with reality.

Less than a month later, Gandhi's "joke" – a 200-mile march to the sea to make illegal salt – had caught the imagination of India and was on the front pages of newspapers around the world.

Making salt was illegal in terms of the Salt Act which prohibited Indians from making salt and forced them to pay tax when they bought it from the government – the sole supplier.

Before the march, Gandhi wrote a letter to the British Viceroy, pointing out the injustice of the tax system – particularly the salt tax – maintained to support an expensive foreign government.

"Take your own salary," Gandhi told the Viceroy. "It is over 21 000 rupees a month. You are getting over 700 rupees a day, against India's average income of less than 2 annas per day. Thus you are getting over 5 000 times India's average income."

Viceroy Lord Irwin had his secretary reply: "His Excellency regrets to learn that you contemplate a course of action which is clearly bound to involve violation of the law and danger to the public peace."

Gandhi, who was 60 years old, commented: "On bended knee I asked for bread, and I received stone instead."

He and 78 men and women from his ashram then set out for the sea on March 12 1930.

Villages through which they passed were decorated in their honour. Between the villages peasants sprinkled water on the road to keep the dust down, and spread petals to make the going easier.

By the time Gandhi got to the coast, several thousand people – including the international press – had joined the march.

After morning prayers on April 6, Gandhi waded into the sea, bathed and purified himself in the Hindu custom, and picked up some salt left by the waves on the beach.

He had defied the Salt Act.

Overnight the country was aroused. Thousands, then tens of thousands swarmed to the beaches to defy the government by making salt. In the cities people staged massive demonstrations at which lumps of illegal salt were sold. Other forms of protest followed, including a boycott of British goods.

Many of the demonstrations were put down by force. There were mass arrests. The jails filled – over 100 000 people were arrested in a matter of weeks.

On May 4 Gandhi was detained without trial "at the pleasure of the government" under a law passed in 1827 by the East India Company.

It was to be another 18 years before India shrugged off British rule, but the Salt March mobilised both the Indian masses and world opinion, setting in motion a process that proved unstoppable.

Gandhi was assassinated at evening prayers soon after India gained independence in 1948. (Based on material from Kumar and Puri: *Mahatma Gandhi, His Life and Influence,* Heinemann, London, 1982)

See also: Satyagraha, Raid

GRAFFITI

Words or drawings scratched, drawn or painted on walls, fences, rocks and other public surfaces, take on special significance in censored and suppressed societies. Political slogans are often turned into graffiti. Occasionally, graffiti become slogans, as in the case of the post-purple police dye: "The purple shall govern".

■ YOU CAN'T WHITEWASH THE WRITING ON THE WALL

THOSE who can't speak through television or radio channels are addressing their audiences on public walls. What we may not read in the newspapers we see around us as graffiti. For instance "SADF Get Out Of Our Townships".

Graffiti, much like the Chinese wall newspapers, also inform and comment on events and experiences. "Hospital Racism is a Sick Practice" appeared after an official statement that the new building at Groote Schuur Hospital would segregate patients according to racial classification.

In Johannesburg, people woke up on the morning of the 1987 "white" election to see "Good morning, lemmings!" spraypainted on a wall.

Mural messages also mobilise mass unity – "Remember June 16", for example. Then there are the regular salutations – "Viva Sayco", "Viva Cosatu", "UDF Lives".

It is probable that much existing graffiti is subdued or subverted by oppositional scribes. The obscenely personal and the politically nonsensical have, of late, become more apparent. "Hang All ANC (later changed to AWB) Scum with Piano Wire" is an example. It also indicates that both sides can play the game and that there are no rules.

Statements are constantly erased or adjusted to suit another point of view: "End Conscription Campaign" became "Every Coward's Choice" which changed again to "Each Comrade's Conscience".

The authorities admit there is not much they can or are prepared to do about "offensive and objectionable" slogans.

– Weekly Mail, 28.1.88

■ DETAINEE'S 'NOT GUILTY' PLEA TO CELL GRAFFITI

A FORMER security detainee has pleaded not guilty to a charge of malicious damage to property for allegedly writing biblical verses and extracts from the Freedom Charter on the newly painted walls and doors of his cell.

Mr Desmond Stevens, 22, of Macassar, was detained at the Strand police station from August 22 to September 15 this year.

Yesterday in the Strand Magistrate's Court his attorney, Ms I Olckers, said her client admitted writing on the walls of cell six with a ballpoint pen he had obtained from a policeman.

The graffiti included eight quotations from the Freedom Charter, eight poems, and Luke 4, verse 18, on the prison door.

Constable Juanita van Rensburg said in evidence that the Strand police station cells, which had had black walls, were painted either beige or grey early in September. Under cross-examination she said she could not say definitely if there were graffiti in other cells, but that cell three – a communal cell used for most prisoners – always had names and obscenities scribbled on its walls.

The matter was postponed to January 10 next year. Bail of R200 was extended.

– The Argus, 15.11.89

HAUNTING

In India in 1928, volunteers followed British officials everywhere, camping on roads outside their official bungalows. More volunteers replaced those who were arrested until the authorities tired of the process.

In the 1950s and 60s, members of the Black Sash used to silently "haunt" cabinet ministers at public places like airports. Many of the officials were embarrassed and would go to great lengths to avoid the protesters.

HOMAGE

Paying tribute or showing public respect can be a means of expressing or encouraging solidarity with a cause. The many honours bestowed on Nelson Mandela, ranging from honorary degrees and the naming of streets and squares (abroad) and schools (in SA, by pupils with paintbrushes), to books on his life ensured that he dominated the SA scene despite his incarceration.

The restoration of the desecrated tombstone dedicated to the 29 people shot dead by police in Uitenhage on March 21 1985, is another example of homage. On the third anniversary of their deaths, mourners unveiled the restored monument, using the occasion to honour other victims of political violence as well.

A memorial service organised by the WPCC to commemorate the tenth anniversary of the martyrdom of Steve Biko on September 12 1977, kept his memory and his cause alive, as do other forms of homage to Biko.

HUNGER STRIKE

The detainees' hunger strike of February 1989 was one of the most successful forms of nonviolent action ever undertaken in SA. It accomplished the release of hundreds of detainees, compelled the authorities to an unprecedented caution about the practice of detention without trial, and may well be seen as ushering in the final, decisive phase of resistance.

■ HUNGER STRIKE VICTORY

– Statement comes from prison: "We are eating again. A major victory has been won."

THE 300 hunger-striking detainees are on the verge of a major victory.

Church leaders emerged from a meeting yesterday with Minister of Law and Order Adriaan Vlok and said that a "substantial number" of detainees would be released in the next fortnight.

They called on the hunger strikers – who have been demanding to be charged or released – to suspend their fast for that period.

According to lawyers, 21 detainees are in hospital, though unofficial reports put the figure as high as 40.

Already yesterday there were hints that Durban prisons were preparing to release up to 50 detainees within the next 24 hours.

Diepkloof, Johannesburg prisoners yesterday released a statement saying they were eating again. "An important victory has been won," they said.

Archbishop Desmond Tutu, one of the churchmen who met the minister, said: "We want to avoid using the language of victory. For us the victory will come when all detainees are released."

However, he added: "A very significant move has occurred through nonviolent action."

Vlok's representative, Brigadier Leon Mellet, said the victory had been negotiation.

However the outcome is described, it is clearly of major significance.

Two weeks ago, the long-term detainees – many of whom have been held for 32 months – had little prospect of release. They had exhausted their legal remedies and were facing the possibility of sitting in prison as long as the state of emergency continued – possibly for years.

Now it appears that most of the 800 –1 000 emergency detainees will be released, though they are likely to be heavily restricted.

Their lawyers have met with Vlok and discussed each individual case – something they have been trying to do since the beginning of the emergency.

The Hunger Strike Support Committee said much had been achieved through the joint efforts of detainees, community organisations, church leaders and lawyers.

– Weekly Mail, 17.2.89

■ ANGER OF A HUNGER STRIKER'S FAMILY

WE, the family of detained human rights lawyer Willie Hofmeyr, feel compelled to make public the following facts:

As a white Afrikaner who has had the courage to stand up and fight for the rights of voteless South Africans, he has become a marked man against whom the State has been waging a 13-year-long vendetta.

He was banned for five years between 1976 and 1981. In 1987 he was detained for two weeks. Last year he was restricted and placed under virtual house arrest from January to May.

From May to October he was imprisoned without charge for five months, most of the time in effective solitary confinement.

Last October, within a few days of bringing a Supreme Court action charging unlawful detention, he was released. He demanded legal costs. The State paid. This speaks for itself.

On release he was again restricted. He decided recently with others to ignore his restriction order. He was twice arrested and brought to court. In both cases the court released him on bail without hearing any charges. He was detained on August 26 under the emergency regulations while acting as a lawyer.

Since this again meant imprisonment without charge or recourse to the courts for an indefinite period, he decided that the only legal means of protest still open to him was to further risk his health and life in a protest fast.

He has now eaten nothing for 10 days. He is extremely emaciated and weak and is in Groote Schuur Hospital under guard. These are the actions of the government which we white voters brought to power. Are we going to do it again?

– *The Argus, 5.9.89*

(Willie Hofmeyr was released seventeen days later, after his family obtained an interim court order forbidding police to chain him to his hospital bed.)

The hunger strike is a form of fast. Like the practice of austerity, fasting has both an inward and an outward power. Gandhi fasted both to purify himself and to touch the conscience of the opponent. Three kinds of fast are distinguished by authorities like Gene Sharp:

1. Hunger strike: Refusing to eat, with the aim of forcing opponents to grant certain demands, but without any serious attempt to "convert" them. This is a method often used by detainees and political prisoners.

2. Satyagrahic fast: The kind of fast often undertaken by Gandhi, whose aim was to sting the conscience of wrongdoers – both the British authorities and resisters who had slipped into undisciplined behaviour.

3. Fast of moral pressure: This type of fast lacks the full "conversion" intent of the satyagrahic fast, but is a conscious attempt to exert moral pressure on the opponent with the aim of achieving certain objectives e.g. the release of children in detention.

An example is the ECC "Fast for a Just Peace" undertaken in September/October1985 and spearheaded by Ivan Toms in Cape Town, Dave Hartman in Grahamstown and Richard Steele in Durban.

In January 1986, a follower of Gandhi, Dr Pankaj Joshi of Laudium in Pretoria, went on a seven-day fast to draw attention to the need for peaceful resolution of the problems facing the country.

Over 100 people joined him in his fast and he received widespread support for a petition calling on the State President to open negotiation with all leaders.

■ A BUDDHIST PRAYS AND FASTS FOR THE CHILDREN

NARA Greenway's passion is the oppressed, the defenceless and the underprivileged.

It was therefore inevitable that the British Buddhist's attention would turn to SA. This week she started a 40-day "prayer-fast" on a rainswept Cape Town sidewalk opposite parliament.

Sister Greenway, ordained as a Buddhist priest of the Nipponzan Myohoji order 12 years ago, said she was fasting to allow her to concentrate totally on "prayers for the children in detention".

Her protest, accompanied by Buddhist chanting and the beating of a drum, has not gone unnoticed by the country's authorities.

She was warned by a policeman earlier this week that she had to have magisterial permission to carry out the fast on the pavement outside the city's famous St George's Cathedral.

The officer also confiscated Free The Children T-shirts worn by two women helping Sister Greenway. He explained that the shirts were forbidden under the state of emergency.

Sister Greenway continued her fast, saying "It is perfectly permissible under the emergency regulations to pray."

– *Sunday Tribune, 17.5.87*

(At the end of her fast, weak and wracked by "the dry heaves", Sister Greenway said the most rewarding moment of her long vigil had been the announcement that 250 children were to be released from detention.)

GUY TILLIM

LEFT
A British Buddhist nun, Nara Greenway, fasts and prays for child detainees in SA in 1988.

IGNORING AUTHORITY

This low-profile form of defiance involves quietly carrying on with one's duties while taking no notice of laws perceived as unjust. Ministers who married couples forbidden to marry by the Prevention of Mixed Marriages Act (abolished in June 1985) were using this method.

■ IT'S MIXING ALL THE WAY

A PRINCIPAL of a white primary school in Woodstock admitted this week that he had "turned a blind eye" when children who were not white applied for admission to his school.

He said, however, that white education officials were trying to put a stop to this practice.

"If I were allowed to I would open the doors of this school tomorrow and let in children of all races," he said.

The principal, who granted the interview on condition that his name was not used, said most principals in the area had the same attitude.

–South, 15.10.87

■ PRINCIPALS LEARN TO 'PLAY THE SYSTEM'

WHITE population growth, in line with trends in the West, shows a decline, and currently stands at 0,5%.

White schools are doing everything to overcome the dearth of pupils, from offering more attractive curricula to giving false figures on pupil numbers and turning a blind eye to "darker-skinned" pupils.

A teacher, who asked not to be named, said: "Principals are learning how to play the system. At the school where I taught, about half the pupils were coloured and Indian.

"The principal makes sure the paperwork is OK, and spends a great deal of time getting kids with one white parent 'reclassified'. Otherwise his job, and those of his staff, are on the line.

"The Transvaal Education Department inspector connives at the whole thing. There seems to be a tacit agreement at official level that it's the only way to keep things running."

– Weekly Mail, 14.7.89

INFORMATION

When the authorities constantly change the rules of repression, nonviolent activists have to keep up – and in fact stay one step ahead of the law. Organisations like UCT's Legal Education and Action Project (LEAP) and the Black Sash have produced clear and simple publications which set out rights and procedures to be followed in case of arrest or detention (e.g. *Police Powers*, Parts 1 to 4, and *The Law Courts and You*).

Another example is an ad placed in the *Weekly Mail* (21.2.86) by Namda under the headline "An Appeal To All Health Professionals", which set out "guidelines for ethical behaviour in situations following civil unrest". It listed patients' rights, suggested steps health workers might take to safeguard those rights, and gave advice on how hospital staff should deal with law enforcement officers.

INTERVENTION

A suffering society can be a volatile society, where violence erupts. The role of the peacemaker who intervenes in such a situation either physically or verbally calls for great courage, as does teaching nonviolence in the face of organised violent revolt.

■ TUTU'S ULTIMATUM

THE Anglican Bishop of Johannesburg and Nobel Peace Prize laureate, Bishop Desmond Tutu, yesterday threatened to pack his bags and leave SA if "suspected enemies" were killed in the manner in which a woman was burnt alive in Duduza township on Saturday.

In an impassioned plea to about 30 000 mourners packed into KwaThema Stadium, Bishop Tutu said: "If you do this kind of thing again, I will find it difficult to speak for the cause of liberation again."

After Bishop Tutu made his plea at the stadium, he led the crowd chanting: "We shall be free."

Bishop Tutu said: "If the violence continues, I will pack my bags, collect my family and leave this beautiful country that I love so passionately and so deeply.

"I want to say to you that I condemn in the strongest possible terms what happened in Duduza on Saturday. I deplore all forms of violence.

"Our cause is just and noble. That is why it is going to prevail and bring victory to us. You cannot use methods to gain the goal of liberation that our enemy will use against us.

"The pictures of that woman being burnt were shown around the world. There are many people around the world who support us. When they saw that woman burning on television, they must have said that maybe we are not ready for freedom. Let us not spoil things by those methods again.

"I want you to demonstrate the discipline of a people that are ready for freedom."

He then asked the crowd to chant after him: "We dedicate ourselves to the freedom struggle for all of us, black and white. We shall be free."

During the funeral service members of the SADF and police patrolled the vicinity of the stadium. When the mourners left the stadium to bury 15 local residents who were shot dead two weeks ago, the SADF and police made their presence seen.

They took up vantage points along the route to the cemetery and near the graveyard. Mourners left the stadium chanting and their ranks swelled to about 40 000 along the 3km route.

After the burial the SADF in troop carriers and police in Casspirs followed various splinter groups that went to the homes of the dead youths' families. There were no apparent scenes of confrontation.

– The Star, 24.7.85

■ BOESAK SAVES ALLEGED POLICE INFORMER

DR ALLAN BOESAK saved an alleged police informer yesterday from an angry crowd who attacked him at a George funeral of three men shot dead by police during recent unrest in the town's Lawaaikamp township.

The man, singled out as a police informer by some mourners at the service at St Paul's Church, had his wife and children with him.

People in the 2 000-strong crowd, which jammed the church and its surrounds, began beating the man.

Dr Boesak, who was scheduled to speak during the funeral, jumped into the throng and shielded the man, then pulled him through the crowd, out of the church, and bundled him and his family into a car and drove off.

Dr Boesak said later: "I don't know if I saved the man's life. I didn't want to see him hurt. I just did what I had to do under the circumstances."

– Sunday Tribune, 2.3.86

JOGGING and JOLLING

When all open-air activities except religious and sporting events are banned, gatherings like picnics, fun runs, sports and festivals become important alternative ways of bringing people together to affirm shared values and hopes.

An additional effect of such gatherings, intended or unintentional, may be to expose the opponents' over-reaction to satire.

■ A SINISTER HORDE OF PUFFING PEACENIKS

THE problem was this: How do you motivate a bunch of unfit intellectuals, paunchy pacifists and flat-footed feminists to jog 5km around Zoo Lake?

The solution was simple: bring the South African Police, preferably the riot squad.

That was the case at the "Run for Peace" at Zoo Lake last Sunday, when the boys in blue provided a breakthrough in sporting medicine that should be noted by anyone trying to organise a fun run for those who find no fun in running.

When lawyer Kathy Satchwell stood up to tell the crowd that the City Council had withdrawn permission for the event, ageing activists who had come as spectators were suddenly shouting "Let's run!"

But the final straw came from the riot squad commander. He took a megaphone and warned the crowd that it constituted an illegal gathering and it had 15 minutes to disperse.

Someone stood up and suggested that the crowd obey the police and disperse at a slow jog along the planned route.

The Run for Peace was on. Now it was no normal run: it had become a major news event.

– Weekly Mail, 6.12.85

■ BRAAIVLEIS, FOOTBALL, PEOPLE'S POWER – AND BOKSBURG LAKE

A LARGE red banner declared: "Hier Kom People's Power" when about 200 people of all races yesterday converged on the "whites only" Boksburg lake for a picnic in defiance of the town council's petty apartheid regulations.

Champagne flowed and the braai smoke filled the air as the jubilant crowd, mostly coloureds from nearby Reiger Park, defiantly occupied the "white man's pleasure resort".

The picnic was organised by the Save Boksburg Committee to coincide with the first anniversary of the entrenchment of petty apartheid laws by the Conservative Party-controlled town council.

"What happens here today is not only a question of having access to the lake but is the overall political effort to change society," said Reiger Park resident Jerry Thuys.

As the picnic got into full gear, youths began toyi-toyi-ing and chanting freedom songs, jumping round in circles.

Banners and posters carried the messages: "All apartheid laws must go", "This lake must be enjoyed by all" and "Mandela the freedom of Boksburg awaits U", hung from the trees and against lakeside poles.

– Weekly Mail, 27.10.89

JOKING

Humour can be used in a conciliatory way with the aim of converting the opponent. During a speech at the conclusion of the triumphant peace march in Cape Town on September 13 1989, Archbishop Desmond Tutu, addressing his remarks to President FW de Klerk, said: "You said you wanted to know if we could be peaceful – come here and see a p-e-a-c-e-f-u-l people!"

Archbishop Tutu then appealed for silence – "Let's just keep quiet!" – and there was a complete hush from the huge crowd. "Mr De Klerk, did you hear a pin drop?" the archbishop asked to a burst of laughter and applause, before continuing: "Mr De Klerk, come and look at technicolour – they tried to make us one colour, purple, but we are the rainbow people, the people of a new South Africa." *(The Argus,* 14.9.89)

Satire can also be a devastating political tool, as was demonstrated during the sandcastle saga that occurred in 1986.

■ POLICE SQUAD STAMPS ON SANDCASTLE PROTEST

STATE of emergency regulations were invoked by police at Clifton's Fourth beach yesterday after about 40 people wearing "Stop the Call-up" T-shirts built a symbolic sandcastle in the shape of Cape Town's Castle.

The castle-building exercise, undertaken by the End Conscription Campaign to highlight the call-up this week of thousands of young South Africans, began at 9.30am.

About 10.30 a beach constable approached the group, asked if they had "permission" to build the sandcastle, and said that members of the public had complained about the group's activities.

Soon afterwards police arrived and told the group they had 10 minutes to take off their T-shirts, knock down the sandcastle and disperse.

– Cape Times, 13.1.86

■ PASOP, MUD PIES COULD BE NEXT

BY now everybody knows that sandcastles can be subversive.

I personally have stopped building them, because I have an innate aversion to breaking the law. I also discourage children from building them on our local beach, explaining to them that they are the innocent and unwitting tools of lawlessness and disorder.

– Cape Times, 14.1.86

■ A POLICY BUILT ON SAND

PLEASE be careful in future about the T-shirt you're wearing when building sandcastles.

Oh, and another friendly warning – be careful not to be an illegal gathering, and the style of sandcastle you choose to build. You've got to get permission to build certain styles. We can't have you being held under the emergency regulations now, can we – just when you're on hols by the sea.

– Argus, 14.1.86

■ THE SANDCASTLE EMERGENCY

LET adults build sandcastles, and soon they would want to build the real thing, thus undermining the state. Fortunately this danger was recognised in time on Sunday, by both a small section of the public and the forces of law and order.

– Cape Times, 15.1.86

■ WHY SANDCASTLES WERE BANNED

HOUSE OF ASSEMBLY. – MPs rocked with mirth yesterday when told police had banned the building of sandcastles on Clifton beach last month.

Explaining why police ordered ECC supporters to stop building sandcastles at Clifton, the Deputy Minister of Law and Order, Mr Adriaan Vlok, said: "Clifton is such a pretty area but they built such large castles that people could not use the seashore."

– Cape Times, 19.2.86

They'll nail anyone who ever scratched his ass during the National Anthem.
– Humphrey Bogart
(speaking of the House Un-American Activities Committee)

JOURNEYS

*J*ourneys, usually on foot, can draw public attention to a political or humanitarian cause, or may have a moral purpose. A pilgrimage may be a penance for some action or policy, or it may be a means of dedicating oneself to a programme for change.

■ TWO MEN GO ON 9-MONTH GOODWILL FOOTSLOG

TWO Springs men – one black, the other white – will soon set out on an epic 8 000km walk around SA to promote goodwill between people in a project called "Reach Out".

This is the first time this has ever been attempted.

The epic walk by Kurt Sartorius, 40, and Isaac Nhlapo, 39, starts in Johannesburg on May 12 and will take about nine months to complete.

The two men will slog it out on foot through desert and wilderness, across rivers and mountains, through dorps and cities. Everywhere they go they will carry goodwill messages to communities which are prepared to reach out to each other.

Sartorius, married with a family, is an accountant who has led several expeditions through South American jungles and mountains. He believes the 8 000km walk will be his greatest challenge.

Nhlapo is a driver for a Johannesburg sporting company. He is also married and has a large family. He took part in the SA Columbia Amazonas expedition led by Sartorius in 1979.

– Sowetan, 30.4.89

■ EIGHT SET OUT ON PROTEST PILGRIMAGE

GRAHAMSTOWN. – Accompanied by the Bishop of Grahamstown, the Rt Rev B B Burnett, eight young men – six priests and two university lecturers – marched through the city today at the beginning of a pilgrimage of almost two months to Cape Town, 914km away.

The pilgrimage is being made to protest against South Africa's migrant labour system and the break-up of African family life.

Among the marchers is the Rev David Russell, who this year lived for six months on rations given to inhabitants of the Dimbaza resettlement camp – as a protest against conditions there.

– The Argus, 16.12.72

(The pilgrimage ended with a service on Rondebosch Common on January 14 1973, and included a newly drafted Charter for Family Life, summarising the message of the pilgrims.)

KEENING

Public weeping can be deeply disturbing to an opponent. "Between the burning of the Crossroads satellite camps and KTC (May-June 1986) about 150 women gathered at St George's Cathedral in Cape Town and decided to march to parliament.

"They unloaded their babies on blankets spread on the ground near the gates of parliament – one mother dumped her baby at the feet of the police at the gates and other mothers followed suit until there was a heap of little babies. The police did not know what to do.

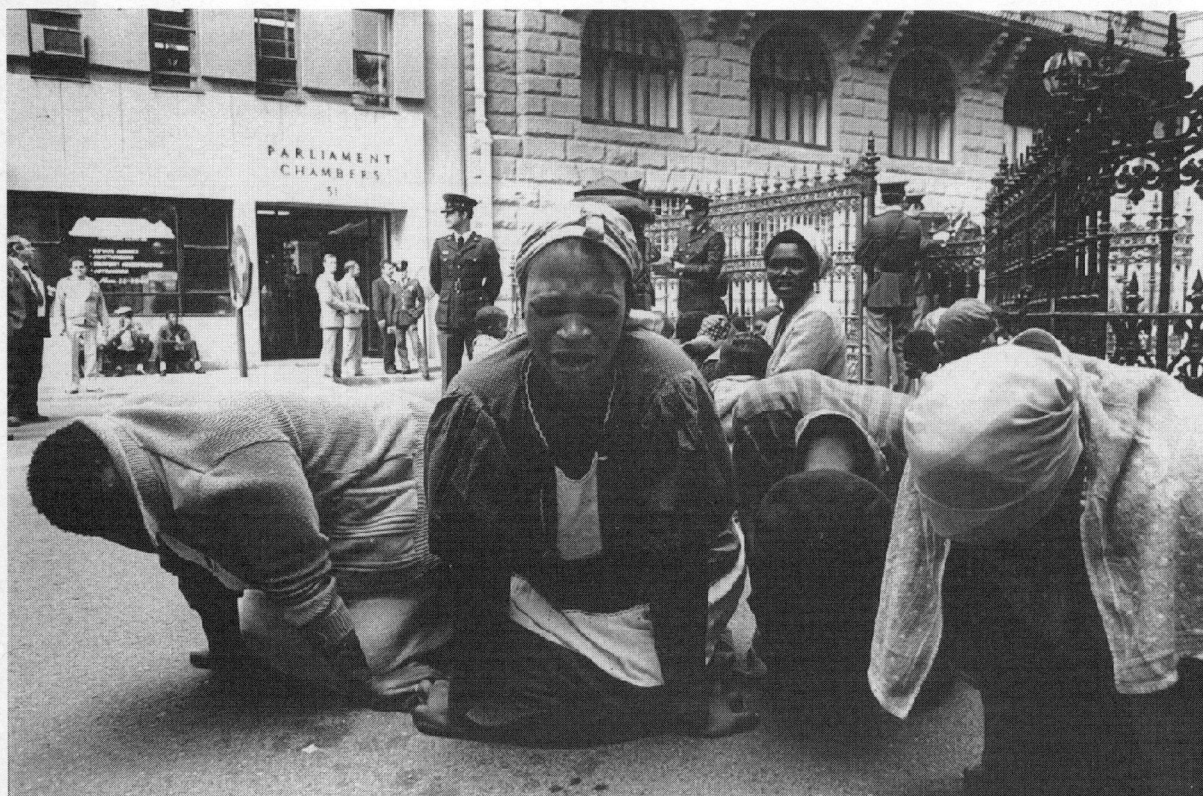

ABOVE
Crossroads women outside parliament in May 1986.

GUY TILLIM

"People began to gather and the women started weeping and wailing – the most awful, eerie and spine-chilling sound.

"The police closed the gates and tried to be reasonable, saying 'No, you can't see the minister!' but they were clearly freaked out by the sound of the sobbing. Police reinforcements arrived and ordered everyone to disperse. The only people who did so were the onlookers, after police charges.

The women carried on keening.

"Only one big police van at a time could get into the narrow alley near the women, who were picked up and loaded one by one into the vans. While this was happening the other women started banging on the sides of the van, saying 'You can put us in prison because we don't have houses anyway.' The women subsequently spent about six hours in the vans outside Caledon Square. They were eventually let out and charged but the charges were dropped some months later. The NVA was very powerful theatre and received wide publicity." *(Verbal account of NV activist and reporter,* 13.1.88*)*

KING

When Martin Luther King was jailed after an anti-segregation protest in Birmingham in 1963, he wrote his *Letter from a Birmingham Jail* in answer to eight white clergymen who denounced him. "I am in Birmingham because injustice is here," he said. "Gandhi said, 'So long as the superstition that men should obey unjust laws exists, so long will their slavery exist.'

"Any law that degrades human personality is unjust. All segregation statutes are unjust because segregation distorts the soul and damages the personality.

"You may well ask: Why direct action? Why sit-ins, marches and so forth? Isn't negotiation a better path? You are quite right in calling for negotiation. Indeed this is the very purpose of direct action.

"Nonviolent direct action seeks to create such a crisis and foster such a tension that a community which has constantly refused to negotiate is forced to confront the issue. It seeks so to dramatise the issue that it can no longer be ignored. We know through painful experience that freedom is never voluntarily given by the oppressor; it must be demanded by the oppressed."

Born on January 15, 1929, in Atlanta, Georgia, King went to university – Morehouse College in Atlanta – at the age of 15, under a special programme for gifted students. An early interest in both law and medicine was eclipsed in his senior year by a decision to enter the ministry.

He graduated from Crozer Theological Seminary, where he was elected president of the student body, in 1951. He earned a doctorate from Boston University in 1955.

He was a Baptist pastor in Montgomery, Alabama, when he was elected president of the Montgomery Improvement Association, formed to fight racism on local buses after Mrs Rosa Parkes was arrested in December 1955 for refusing to move to the "black" end of a bus. The buses were desegregated after a year-long boycott led by King.

The Montgomery campaign was followed by the formation of the Southern Christian Leadership Conference, which gave King a base of operation throughout the South and a national platform. In 1960 he moved to his native city of Atlanta, where he became co-pastor with his father of the Ebenezer Baptist Church.

He was arrested in October 1960 with 33 other protesters in Atlanta. Charges were dropped but King was jailed on the pretext that he had violated probation on a minor traffic offence. He was released after John F Kennedy intervened, an action many thought contributed to Kennedy's slender election victory eight days later. On August 28 1963, King was one of the leaders of a march on Washington by over 200 000 people demanding equal justice for all citizens. This was the occasion of his famous "I have a dream" speech, celebrated 26 years later on a banner displayed in St George's Cathedral on the day of the great Cape Town peace march.

The following year the Civil Rights Act was passed, outlawing discrimination in employment and public facilities, and King won the Nobel Peace Prize.

Accepting the prize, King said: "Negroes in the US, following the people of

BELOW
Martin Luther King addresses a crowd during the Civil Rights Campaign in the 1950s.

India, have demonstrated that nonviolence is not sterile passivity, but a powerful and moral force which makes for social transformation. I accept this award today with an abiding faith in America and an audacious faith in the future of mankind. I refuse the cynical notion that nation after nation must spiral down a militaristic stairway into the hall of nuclear destruction. I believe that unarmed truth and unconditional love will have the final word in reality. I still believe that we shall overcome."

For the next five years, King battled both to broaden the struggle to include concerns other than racism – poverty and the Vietnam war, for instance – and to counter tactical opposition, and derision, from young militants. On April 4 1969, he was killed by a sniper's bullet.

Since 1986, a national holiday has been observed in his honour in the US on the third Monday in January.

See also: Gandhi, Satyagraha

KNEELING

Demonstrators sometimes sit down when challenged by police. Since such action was often likely to be met with teargas, sjamboks and mass arrests, some protesters chose to kneel instead of sit. This more humble posture did not protect demonstrating clerics in Cape Town from police water cannon in February 1988 but it had some success in Zwelethemba in 1985.

■ GO AWAY, THE WOMEN BEG POLICE

NEARLY 400 residents of the small Western Cape township of Zwelethemba, near Worcester, made a dramatic appeal to riot police this week to withdraw from their township.

Late on Sunday afternoon, the residents marched towards a police roadblock at the edge of the township and then fell to their knees and pleaded with the police to go.

The marchers, most of them women, carried placards saying, "We don't fight. Take the policemen away from the township."

The women waited in silence as three police officers walked towards them.

As a representative of the marchers gave details of the community's grievances to Worcester's district commandant, Lieutenant-Colonel J A Swart, heavily armed reinforcements brought in hurriedly from Worcester kept guard a few metres away.

When the discussions were over, the woman asked the people, who had been joined by throngs of curious youth, to turn back. The commanding officer also signalled his men to withdraw from their positions.

– Weekly Mail, 23.8.85

LETTERS

Letters as a method of protest and persuasion can take several forms. They may be private letters to the person or body responsible for an unsatisfactory state of affairs. They may be "open" letters, written to a particular person but sent to the correspondence pages of newspapers, where their message reaches the general public, so focusing the glare of publicity on the recipient.

The greater the number of people who sign a letter, the more effect it can have; and the more prominent these people are, the greater its potential impact. However, a simple letter from the heart can be eloquent and effective in making a political point.

■ GIVE US BACK OUR BROTHER, MR VLOK

Dear Editor,
I am writing this letter to the Minister of Law and Order, Adriaan Vlok, to bring to his attention the plight of my brother Zandisile Isaac Gojela.

Zandisile was detained the week after the state of emergency was declared. He has spent more than 18 months in detention without trial. I think it is unfair and barbaric to keep someone behind bars for so long without bringing him to court. We, the members of his family, desperately need to have him with us.

We have just spent Christmas without him. And because he is detained, he was not able to attend his father's burial.

The reason I am publishing this in *New Nation* is that I wrote to the minister in October last year, and never received a reply.

DUGARD GOJELA, Zwide.

– New Nation, 11.2.88

In December 1985, Tongaat-Hulett group chairman Chris Saunders wrote a letter to his 43 000 employees, outlining the political stance of the group's management.

He said the group was an economic unit, not a political party, but had a strong interest in political reform "which is therefore indirectly also in the interest of all employees". Among the reforms he listed as necessary in the view of management were: the lifting of the state of emergency, an end to detention without trial, the abolition of all discriminatory laws and full citizenship rights for all. (*Natal Mercury,* 14.12.85)

In October 1987, president of the World Alliance of Reformed Churches Dr Allan Boesak wrote an open letter to school pupils which was published in *South* (29.10.87). "Hi kids," the letter began, "I am writing these few lines to you as a message of encouragement and to tell you about the importance of being an educated person."

Dr Boesak went on to say that education was "one of the mightiest weapons you and I have to change things" and to urge children to do their best to serve their communities.

LIGHT

When Albert Luthuli, ANC president and later recipient of the Nobel Peace Prize, called off the Defiance Campaign in 1953, he appealed to ANC members and sympathisers to light bonfires, candles or lanterns outside their houses "as a symbol of the spark of freedom which we are determined to keep alive in our hearts, and as a sign to freedom-lovers that we are keeping the vigil on that night".

Although there have been times when the lights in SA have burnt low, the spark has never been extinguished.

■ POLICE POUNCE UPON THE DASTARDLY CANDLE-CRAZIES

LIGHTING a candle has become a political decision in Cape Town this Christmas. Candlelight vigils have been held every Wednesday night since the beginning of December in the black and coloured suburbs, in sympathy with and support for detainees and in protest against the detention system itself.

The vigils have been tremendously effective. So effective, in fact, that Brigadier Chris Swart, Western Cape's divisional police commissioner, decided they were "deliberately aimed at stirring up people's emotions, which leads them to violent acts".

So the police moved against the lighters of candles in a sjambok-wielding show of force. Candles have been wrenched from the hands of inoffensive citizens, teargas has been fired.

A candlelight procession in Sea Point was broken up and a candlelight carol service scheduled for the Day of the Vow in Athlone was banned as an illegal gathering. Three people were detained for taking part in candlelight services.

Tonight's Carols by Candlelight service at Kirstenbosch has been called off because the Anglican rector will not ask permission to hold the service.

– Weekly Mail, 20.12.85

ANNA ZIEMINSKI

RIGHT
A candlelight vigil was organised by women's organisa-tions in St Mary's Cathedral, Johan-nesburg, to mark a 1 000 days of the state of emergency.

An inside view of the Cape Town candlelight campaign of late 1985 is given by an activist : "The campaign – switching off lights and lighting candles between 7pm and 9pm (8pm in some places) on Wednes-days – began as an action in solidarity with those killed in the Trojan Horse inci-dent (15.10.85).

"It became a campaign of protest against the state of emergency.

"Activists visited the Athlone area beforehand and in the first week the cam-paign worked well in almost the whole area visited. By the second week it had spread to a whole lot of other areas.

"The Belgravia Road area remained the centre of the campaign and hundreds of cars came there on Wednesday nights, jamming the road solid for about 3km.

"Thousands of people came out of their houses to stand in the road. Crowds toyi-toyied round the block, impromptu mass meetings were held. The police tried to get in but could not get through the traffic jam. It was enormously successful, lasting seven to eight weeks, mobilising people, attracting publicity."

MARCHES

Freedom went on the march in 1989, in Eastern Europe and in South Africa. As millions mobilised, this method of protest and persuasion proved itself in a spectacular way. It brought down the Berlin Wall, caused communist governments to collapse, and in SA marked the moment when the state could no longer curb the expression of the will of the people.

■ MARCH FOR PEACE: TUTU, MAYOR LEAD 30 000 IN MASSIVE PROTEST

IN Cape Town's largest protest march in 29 years, nearly 30 000 people yesterday filled five city streets from St George's Cathedral to the City Hall without incident and without a single uniformed policeman in attendance.

The historic march, tightly controlled by Mass Democratic Movement marshals, brought most of the central business district to a standstill as a mass of humanity spread 1,5km down Wale, Adderley, Strand, Buitenkant and Darling streets.

It followed a week of turbulence and unrest in the Western Cape and was the first legal demonstration in a decade within earshot of parliament despite several laws banning such gatherings and the three-year-old state of emergency.

The crowd was initially led by Anglican Archbishop Desmond Tutu, World Alliance of Reformed Churches president Dr Allan Boesak, newly elected Mayor Mr Gordon Oliver, Muslim Judicial Council president Sheikh Nazeem Mohamed, and rector of the University of the Western Cape Professor Jakes Gerwel.

Hundreds of chanting township youths soon surged to the front.

The procession – which rivalled that of 1960 when PAC activist Mr Philip Kgosana led 30 000 people from Langa to Caledon Square police station without major incident – was briefly stalled by a barrage of media crews barring the way.

Besides the mayor, participants included senior Democratic Party members, rectors and vice-chancellors of the Peninsula's major tertiary institutions, and leading churchmen and businessmen.

The acting chief magistrate of Cape Town, Mr HS van Wyk, yesterday morning gave permission for the march despite organisers not having applied.

– Cape Times, 14.9.89

Courtesy of THE ARGUS

ABOVE

**A peaceful march
in Cape Town on
September 13
1989.**

PEACEFUL PROTEST IS BACK ON THE AGENDA

CAPE Town's watershed march has notched an unprecedented victory for the Mass Democratic Movement and put peaceful protest firmly back on South Africa's political agenda.

Within hours of Wednesday's triumphant procession plans were being laid in Grahamstown and Johannesburg for similar actions, part of a groundswell of political confidence.

As Archbishop Desmond Tutu and Dr Allan Boesak addressed the jubilant crowd from the city hall balcony festooned with the ANC colours and the UDF flag, an old man commented: "The National Party will never be able to stop the march to freedom now."

He was a young man during the 1950s, when the ANC regularly held open-air meetings on Cape Town's Grand Parade until its banning in 1960. Now, 30 years later, he was witnessing a long-fought-for renaissance. After three years under a state of emergency, more than 35 000 people had come to register their protest.

A significant political concession had been extracted from the state: the march had been sanctioned by acting State President FW de Klerk.

Addressing the exuberant crowd, Dr Boesak said: "By saying we can march in defiance of his own law we've got De Klerk to defy also."

The march made nonsense of the state of emergency, he added.

Cosatu general secretary Jay Naidoo said: "We have liberated Cape Town today, the task facing us is to make that liberation permanent."

Cape Town's newly installed mayor, Gordon Oliver, whose participation made civic history, was greeted with resounding applause and cries of "Long live the mayor" when he rose and said: "Today Cape Town has won, today we all have the freedom of the city."

As people started to sing Nkosi Sikelel' iAfrika before dispersing, a lawyer said: "We have broken the back of the emergency. How will they ever be able to justify police ever again breaking up a peaceful protest?"

– Weekly Mail, 15.9.89

■ 2 000 MARCH IN GRAHAMSTOWN

GRAHAMSTOWN. – About 2 000 Rhodes University students, academics, clerics and workers, and members of the Grahamstown community took part in a mass protest march through the streets of the city yesterday.

– Cape Times, 15.9.89

■ THOUSANDS JOIN JOBURG MARCH

JOHANNESBURG. – A hard core of about 8 000 people yesterday took part in a colourful protest march in central Johannesburg against election-night killings in the Cape Peninsula.

Police estimated, however, that the crowd later swelled to between 15 000 and 18 000.

After the 50-minute, four-kilometre march from St Mary's Cathedral to John Vorster Square police station to hand over a memorandum for Minister of Law and Order Mr Adriaan Vlok, SA Council of Churches general-secretary the Rev Frank Chikane hailed the event as "a great day for us and a victory for peace".

Permission for the march was granted by Johannesburg's acting Chief Magistrate, Mr Pieter Theron, only when a church service at St Mary's which preceded the march was under way.

Mr Chikane said permission from the magistrate was not asked for.

– Cape Times, 19.9.89

■ THOUSANDS MARCH IN OUDSTHOORN, DURBAN

TENS of thousands of marchers took to the streets of Durban and Oudtshoorn yesterday to protest against government policies in marches unmarred by violence.

In Durban more than 20 000 protesters marched through the city's streets in a legal march and congregated at Durban City Hall.

And in Oudtshoorn, at least 5 000 singing and dancing people from the town's two townships choked the conservative Karoo town's streets, carrying ANC flags and placards to deliver petitions to the local town clerk and police chief.

– Cape Times, 23.9.89

■ 30 000 MARCH IN EAST LONDON

EAST LONDON. – More than 30 000 people participated in a legal march for peace, justice and freedom along Oxford Street here yesterday.

Participants began congregating at 11.40am outside the St John's Anglican Church in Lower Oxford Street.

The start of the march, which followed a short church service, was delayed for some time as marshals escorted clergy to the front of the procession.

The procession, which stretched across four traffic lanes and two parking lanes, was about a kilometre long. It was led by Anglican Bishop David Russell of Grahamstown.

– Cape Times, 28.9.89

■ 7 500 WALK PEACEFULLY IN KIMBERLEY PROTEST

KIMBERLEY. – Close to 7 500 protesters marched peacefully in a disciplined crowd to the Transvaal Road police station from Galeshewe in Kimberley yesterday. The colourful crowd handed a list of grievances to Galeshewe mayor Mr H T Bosvark.

– Cape Times, 29.9.89

■ 20 000 MARCH IN EAST CAPE

KING WILLIAM'S TOWN. – An estimated 20 000 people flooded the town centre here yesterday in the largest peaceful protest march seen in the small town.

Police said no incidents were reported in the march from Holy Trinity Church through the town centre to security police headquarters, where a statement of protest was read and handed over.

A handful of whites joined the marchers, estimates of whose number ranged from 15 000 to 20 000.

– Cape Times, 30.9.89

■ 50 000 MARCH NEAR BLOEMFONTEIN

JOHANNESBURG. – More than 50 000 people thronged the streets of Botshabelo, near Bloemfontein, yesterday to protest against the incorporation of the township into the Qwa Qwa homeland.

The demonstration started at a local church and wound its way to the local magistrate's court where a petition was handed in.

Protesters, holding aloft banners from local organisations as well as Cosatu, Nactu and the ANC, sang, chanted and toyi-toyied as they were monitored by police in several vehicles and hippos.

The co-ordinator of a local advice office, Mr Benny Kotsoane, said they had told residents in the township, which accommodates close on 500 000 people, that they should not be coerced into a confrontation with police.

– Cape Times, 2.10.89

UITENHAGE MARCH BIGGEST IN SA HISTORY

PORT ELIZABETH. – What was perhaps the biggest protest march in SA history took place in the small industrial town of Uitenhage yesterday.

The peaceful march was organised by the MDM, Cosatu, church groups and various other community-based organisations to protest against amendments to the Labour Relations Act.

The size of the crowd was estimated to range from 30 000 earlier in the day to as many as 85 000.

A list of marchers' demands was handed to the divisional inspector of the police in Uitenhage, Brigadier JA Botha, to pass on to the Minister of Law and Order, Mr Adriaan Vlok. Another list of demands was handed to the town's chief magistrate.

No workers reported for work at the Volkswagen or Goodyear factories, and other businesses had a high absentee rate.

– Cape Times, 12.10.89

A factor in the success of the marches of 1989 was the new approach of President FW de Klerk, who intervened effectively to suspend the laws and emergency measures prohibiting such demonstrations. Not one uniformed policeman was to be seen during the landmark Cape Town march.

Thirty years earlier, a crowd of 30 000 – mainly migrant workers – was met by a massive show of force including troops with fixed bayonets outside parliament and machine-gun emplacements in its grounds.

Thousands of lives hung in the balance as the Minister of Justice instructed the police colonel in charge of the security forces to send in armoured cars against the marchers. A peaceful outcome was accomplished because one man obeyed his conscience and another honoured his commitment to nonviolence.

A MARCH OF BETRAYAL – AND OF A MIRACLE

"MASS march to city by 30 000" the headlines ran just under 30 years ago, giving little indication of how narrowly Cape Town had escaped a bloodbath. The key actors in the day's events were a police officer, Brigadier Terry Terblanche (then colonel and head of the Cape Town police) who disobeyed an order from the Minister of Justice, Mr Frans Erasmus; and the regional secretary of the now banned Pan Africanist Congress, Mr Philip Kgosana.

It was March 30, 1960, just nine days after 69 pass law protesters had been shot in Sharpeville. It was also the day a state of emergency was declared.

Brigadier Terblanche, whose promotion came at the age of 84 after his retirement, referred to the day as "the miracle of March 30" until his death. For Mr Kgosana, then a 21-year-old commerce student at UCT, the day ended in betrayal and arrest.

Two groups came into town that day, one on foot from Langa along De Waal Drive, bringing traffic to a standstill. They were asked to wait below Vredehoek by their leader.

From 11am the other group started congregating in Buitenkant Street, having come into town by train and by bus.

Brigadier Terblanche was outside Caledon Square addressing this tense but peaceful and silent crowd, asking for a leader to speak to, when he was called inside to take a phone call from the Minister of Justice.

Only after his death did he give details of that phone call in a statement attached to his will.

He said Mr Erasmus instructed him to send in armoured vehicles.

This order was given despite Brigadier Terblanche's assurances that the situation was under control and that it would be highly dangerous to take the step.

"When I told him I was also in full control of the security of the parliament buildings, his response was 'Carry out my instructions'," the brigadier said.

They were instructions he was unable to follow.

In an interview before his death, Brigadier Terblanche completed the story: "After the call I went outside and a miracle took place."

The miracle was a chance encounter with a man who had worked as a cook under Brigadier Terblanche at Wynberg.

The cook had been assaulted by a constable in the mess and the brigadier had imposed the maximum penalty on the policeman. The cook approached the brigadier and said: "I will never forget you."

It was the cook who told the brigadier that Mr Kgosana was waiting with another crowd at the Roeland Street fire station. Mr Kgosana was sent for and the crowd followed him.

For half an hour the two spoke in the street.

In a recent interview, Mr Kgosana recalled: "When we arrived at Caledon Square, I told Terblanche that I did not want to talk to the police because they had let our people down. They had just killed people in Sharpeville and Langa and they had also arrested our leaders."

Brigadier Terblanche's recall was that Mr Kgosana was "a ball of nerves at first, shaking like a leaf in his short pants".

The outcome of the meeting was an agreement that Mr Kgosana would persuade his people to return home peacefully while the brigadier would secure a meeting with the Minister of Justice that afternoon.

The crowd dispersed in silence at 2pm after they were told by Mr Kgosana of the assurance. He was then lifted shoulder-high and led the demonstrators back to Langa.

But when the young man, still dressed in his blue shorts, returned that afternoon with two companions, he was arrested on the orders of Mr Erasmus.

It was an act of betrayal that deeply disturbed Brigadier Terblanche. "I felt like a traitor. It stamped me as breaking my promise," he said.

Mr Kgosana was held in detention for nine months, eventually charged with incitement and slipped out of the country in 1962 while on bail.

He completed his education abroad and worked as an economist for the UN's Children Emergency Fund in Uganda and Sri Lanka. Last year he was appointed deputy defence secretary of the PAC.

In 1987, when the brigadier's belated promotion was announced, Mr Kgosana said in an interview from Colombo: "All that mattered to me then was that when a promise had been made it was not honoured by the government of SA.

"I believe at Terblanche's level, a policeman, he was only carrying out the order of a minister. I don't think, as much as I opposed him, that he can consider himself a traitor."

– *The Argus, 15.9.89*

Author and journalist Joseph Lelyveld describes the 1960 march as the "hour in which the Bastille might have been stormed in SA and wasn't". Asking why it wasn't, he identifies the doctrine of nonviolence that underlay the thinking of PAC leader Robert Sobukwe, who "felt there was a force and courage latent in the black masses" and that the ANC had not dared enough with its Defiance Campaign of the 1950s.

Sobukwe initiated the PAC's anti-pass law campaign by offering himself for arrest at Orlando police station five hours before the Sharpeville shootings. He wanted Africans to stop carrying passes, present themselves for mass arrests, fill the jails and withhold their labour until the pass laws were abolished.

Sobukwe subsequently spent nine years in prison and was then silenced by a banning order until his death in 1978. In Cape Town, however, Philip Kgosana carried his banner.

In a speech in Langa the day before the campaign started, Kgosana told a mass meeting that the anti-pass campaign was the beginning of a new order that would be compelled by united black action.

It was "the hour for service, sacrifice and suffering", he said. Africans had to promise themselves that they would never carry passes again.

Half his speech was devoted to final instructions from Sobukwe – the last time the PAC leader's words could legally be heard in public.

"Those words became the basis for Sobukwe's eventual conviction for incitement," Lelyveld writes, "yet what he was inciting to was ABSOLUTE NON-VIOLENCE.

"The words were capitalised in Sobukwe's text. Allowing the campaign to degenerate into violence would be to alienate the masses by using them as cannon-fodder, he said.

"After a few days, when we have buried our dead and made moving graveside speeches and our emotions have settled again, the police will round up a few people and the rest will go back to their passes."

What Sobukwe envisaged instead was "a never-ending stream" of nonviolent campaigns until "independence" was achieved. "We are not leading corpses to a new Africa," he declared.

Interpreting Sobukwe's instructions to the Langa crowd, Kgosana made it clear that the command of "absolute nonviolence" meant that defiance extended only to not carrying passes and staying away from work. Orders to disperse were to be obeyed. "Not leading corpses to a new Africa" meant limiting the possibility of police violence.

"If a police officer wants us to disperse, we shall disperse," Kgosana said. Even if leaders were arrested, "the president's order is that you peacefully disperse without making any noise or interjections. You go home, sit in your houses, and paint the house or dig the garden or even play drafts."

Lelyveld believes this speech provides an explanation for "the astonishing denouement of the march eleven days later".

Where Sobukwe went wrong, he concludes, was "to underestimate both the weapon of nonviolent resistance and the ruthlessness of the state".

"He was not, in fact, a Gandhian; he did not believe in forcing the regime to show its violent face to itself and the world, possibly because he knew he had not adequately prepared his followers for what that would mean in South Africa. So he hoped for a miracle." *(Move Your Shadow,* Michael Joseph, London, 1986)

MOTORCADE

A variation of the march, this action involves participants driving cars in a procession, usually at a very slow speed. The cars sometimes carry banners and posters and the motorcade may be accompanied by marchers on foot.

The fleet of small two-stroke-engined cars that crossed the Berlin Wall for celebration trips in November 1989 constituted a spontaneous motorcade. Many flashed their lights and honked their modest horns as they crossed.

■ JOYFUL END TO BOKSBURG BOYCOTT

BOKSBURG. – A year-long boycott of white shops here, conducted in protest at the reimposition of petty apartheid, ended in a joyful mood on Saturday when more than 800 coloured residents of Reiger Park mounted a car cavalcade into the city's commercial area.

Packed buses, cars and vans – many draped with colourful posters and banners – were led by members of the Save Boksburg Committee, the organisation that staged the protest, into the city centre, where they alighted, shook hands with managers of shops and browsed about.

"This is our victory day. We have shown that we cannot be taken for granted. We have been on this defiance campaign for little more than a year. And with the people fully behind us, we have shown that we will not bow down to the dictates of the Conservative Party-controlled town council," said a jubilant Mr Danny Cassell, a leading member of the committee's executive.

Scores of shoppers, wearing a variety of political T-shirts, were greeted by smiling managers who earlier had placed signs in their windows welcoming back the Reiger Park residents.

No incidents were reported, despite the CP council refusing to back down on harsher apartheid in the city. However, it is virtually powerless in the face of the announcement by President FW de Klerk that the Separate Amenities Act would be repealed as soon as possible.

– Cape Times, 20.11.89

MUSIC

Musicians like Bob Dylan and Joan Baez played a leading role in expressing the dissent of the "Woodstock" generation, part of a tradition of musical activism that has been continued and extended by performers in the 1980s. The fund-raising drive for famine-struck Africa led by Bob Geldof is one example, the concert staged at London's Wembley Stadium for Nelson Mandela's 70th birthday, where exiled Miriam Makeba and other stars sang for 80 000 people (and 600-million TV viewers across the world), another.

If musicians have become activists, activists have always been singers, and singing can be a potent form of nonviolent action – both in itself, as an expression of protest and group solidarity, and as a means of "drowning" unwanted speeches or procedures.

There are few better examples of the power of music as than the history and status of the hymn Nkosi Sikelel' iAfrika, regarded as a national anthem by the majority of the people of South Africa, and adopted as a national anthem by Zambia, Tanzania and Zimbabwe. Begun by Klipspruit schoolteacher Enoch Sontonga, who died in 1897, it was completed in 1927 by another teacher, the poet Samuel E Mqhayi.

Initially popularised by school and church choirs, this "song from a heavy heart" – as Cape leader DDT Jabavu called it – came to be sung at the end of all ANC meetings. Many other organisations followed suit and this is still the practice today, notably at political meetings, political funerals and other serious occasions.

◼ A SINGING CROWD ARRIVES FOR THE TRIAL OF THE SINGING WORKERS

HUNDREDS of singing workers rode the trains yesterday to attend a trial of 47 colleagues charged with . . . disturbing the peace by singing on the trains.

More than 500 workers from Johannesburg boarded the 8am train to Kempton Park, singing and chanting, to attend the trial of the 47 workers arrested in June.

On their arrival, the huge crowd was dispersed with sjamboks by a combined force of several members of the SAP, traffic officers who blocked their only escape route, and municipal police. At least 15 were injured.

`And the original 47 accused who were due to appear were inexplicably reduced to 27 when the trial – minus the trialists – was brought before the magistrate. The case was postponed.

More than 450 people have been arrested since June – plus another 100 yesterday morning on the East Rand, a fact communicated to the workers down the seven coaches they occupied as they sang their way east.

When the case was called, two policemen read out the names of those who would appear in three separate cases later this year. Only 27 names were on the list. Sam Rikhotso was one who escaped prosecution, but he was not too happy about the turn of events. "Why is the case against me being dropped?" he asked. "Also, I have questions to ask the court. Now I will carry on singing."

With the "singing trial" postponed, the workers filtered back to the station, where they boarded a train – and sang all the way back to Johannesburg.

– *Weekly Mail, 11.8.89*

Music, thank God, moves us towards Utopia!
– Grace Slick

Courtesy of WELMA ODENDAAL

**RIGHT
Johannes
Kerkorrel in
concert at Pretoria
University in April
1989.**

'SIT DIT AF, SIT DIT AF' SAYS KERKORREL

JOHANNES Kerkorrel, alias Ralph Rabie, explains in his soft, peaceful voice: "The so-called alternative Afrikaners – whoever they might be – have crawled out of the woodwork. All the old rebels are surfacing at our concerts.

"We were always the bottom of the barrel in any case. We realise that many of the problems in our country over the last 40 years are thanks to the National Party and our Afrikaner people. But we are angry about it. We are enraged, because our parents f....d everything up."

Kerkorrel believes that music can change people's attitudes. "You must push your audience a little every time," he says. "You must get them to the point where they see clearly how laughable the paranoia about the ANC is – that paranoia must be sent up and I want to do that.

"I want young people, Afrikaans youth, to learn to know freedom. People have never thought that Afrikaans youth are not free, but they are ultimately absolutely unfree. They are meant to be carrying forward the oppression here, jy weet. They have to shoot at the people and they hate it. They can't take it. That's why people go so crazy when they hear rock and roll."

The sharpest criticism of the music of Kerkorrel and Andre Letoit has come from those who say it is too negative, too anarchistic; that, in Jennifer Ferguson's words, they are just teenage rebels. They cite as an example Kerkorrel's playful song "Almal moet gerook raak/hoog soos 'n spook raak".

In a recent interview with the music magazine *Blits,* Kerkorrel emphatically denies this and says: "I'm really not a destructive person. Anarchy and satire must be used cleverly. You must use it like a surgeon, you must apply it to precisely the right place. People like us have kept quiet for too long. I say we must live for our land, work to change it into something worthwhile – but not with guns."

– Die Suid-Afrikaan, June 1989

NAMING

When people rename themselves and their institutions, their towns and even their countries, they recreate themselves in their own image – a first step to restructuring society.

◼ SWABBING OUT THE TOWNSHIP PAST

MEN wielding paint brushes and carrying pails of paint are busy removing the names of leaders of the outlawed ANC and SACP from the walls of black schools.

The names – Nelson Mandela, Oliver Tambo, Walter Sisulu and Joe Slovo – were painted on the walls by young activists in township classrooms in the past two years.

Emblazoned on school walls in townships around Johannesburg, they signalled a bid to rename the schools after them in recognition of their fight against the established order.

The men armed with swabs were ordered into action after a visit to black schools in Alexandra by the Deputy Minister of Education and Training, Sam de Beer. It was as if he were trying to wipe the slate clean . . . to begin again at the beginning.

– Weekly Mail, 16.1.87

◼ MISSIONARY NAMES

A CHILD was born and it was a boy. The family was so happy that it was a boy because the family name would live on. At the feast they named him Motlagosebatho and they all accepted the name.

His parents were devoted Christians. The child had to be baptised. The pastor refused to accept the right name of the child, saying to the parents that they must give their child a "Christian name".

He then quoted a name from the Bible. The name was Moses. It was to be a so-called Christian name for the boy . . . .

Motlagosebatho visited the pass office to collect his dompas. He tried to use his right name because he was proud of it, but the white man yelled at him, saying "I don't want your kaffir name but your Christian name", and refused to attend to Motlagosebatho.

My fellow brothers and sisters, use your names and stop renaming your progeny. BE PROUD OF YOUR NAME.

– Zamani, Lutheran Youth, Youth Express, Grassroots, 1987

NO-GO ZONES

No-go zones are usually strife-torn areas rendered inaccessible by violence. Cape Town's District Six is something remarkable: a nonviolent no-go zone. It is a monument to the moral outrage of the city's residents (and to the method of non-cooperation). Its desolate landscape makes as strong a political statement as anything ever uttered, written or sung by the novelists, playwrights and musicians who have celebrated District Six.

District Six was declared white on February 11 1966, and some 30 000 people became subject to forced removal. Their resistance, coupled with the outrage of the wider community, made the area a no-go zone for over 20 years.

Despite subsidies and other incentives, few would move into the area to occupy renovated houses or develop new properties. Companies that tried to do so found themselves under pressure, and withdrew. A city councillor with professional architectural interests in a District Six project was compelled to abandon those interests or forfeit election as mayor.

The Anglican Church successfully resisted expropriation and the Moravian Church complex was declared a national monument. A few mosques also held out and large crowds flock to them for Friday prayers and religious festivals.

In 1981 the President's Council declared that District Six "had always been inhabited by coloured people since the emancipation of the slaves and is considered by them as the birthplace of their people". A fifth of the area was subsequently reproclaimed "coloured residential".

By the mid 1980s, Cape Town City Council had installed services (roads, water, etc) and some private sector development was taking place in the renamed Zonnebloem. Much of the area still remains empty, however.

In July 1988 the Hands Off District Six Committee convened a conference in District Six, reaffirming that the area was regarded as "salted earth". The committee opposed a proposal by BP South Africa to finance redevelopment of the land as an "open" area.

The declaration of District Six as a "free settlement area" by President FW de Klerk in November 1989 was met with little enthusiasm by the people of Cape Town, although one family evicted decades before bought a house.

Cape Town city councillor Mr Arthur Wienburg said the decision was "totally unacceptable", while former parish priest of the area Father Basil van Rensburg described it as "an abomination of abominations". "Nobody should tread that sacred soil until the entire Group Areas Act has been repealed," he said. *(The Argus,* 10.10.85; *Weekly Mail,* 8.7.88; *Cape Times* 25.11.89)

OBSTRUCTION

This method of intervention can range from withholding access across land, to interposing oneself between security forces or machines and the people or places they threaten.

The latter depends for success on large numbers of people taking part, as in the Philippine crisis (see *Zabalaza*). However, individuals can achieve a considerable moral victory by risking almost certain arrest and possible injury or death to lay their bodies on the line.

■ OWNER BANS WHITES-ONLY RIDING SCHOOL FROM LAND

A NOORDHOEK landowner has barred the "whites only" Sunbird Riding School from using an access path on his property, after the stables recently refused admission to a visiting computer expert on racial grounds.

The owner, Mr E J (Junior) van der Horst, said yesterday that he had informed the stables in writing "that they are no longer permitted to cross my land".

He said the school had used his land as an access route to Noordhoek beach but would "now have to use the public road".

Meanwhile, Mr Daulat Rai, 34, the man at the centre of the controversy, got his ride on a private farm yesterday.

He said he realised now that "not everybody" in SA held the same views as those of Sunbird Riding School.

– *Cape Times, 24.10.87*

■ SQUATTERS: PRIEST AND TWO OTHERS HELD

THREE whites were arrested at the Modderdam squatter camp today. Police said they had apparently lain down in front of a bulldozer in an attempt to stop the demolitions.

But demolitions went ahead as more shacks were mysteriously set alight. Peninsula Bantu Affairs Administration Board officials said the rest of the shacks would probably be razed by the end of the day.

Police are enforcing a ban on public meetings in the area.

A senior police spokesman confirmed the arrest of the Rev David Russell, assistant priest at the Anglican Church of the Holy Cross at Nyanga, Mr Richard de Satga, who is employed by Shawco, SA Volunteer Services and Envirac, and Mr Michael Poppleton.

The spokesman said he was told the three had been warned that they were trespassing on state property and had been asked to leave.

They had ignored the request and lain down in front of a bulldozer. They had then been arrested and would probably be charged with trespassing.

A woman at the scene early today said she had seen four policemen carrying Mr Russell from the camp.

About 100 whites threatened yesterday to form a human barrier to stop the bulldozers but early today only about 12 were there.

– The Argus, 11.8.77

OCCUPATION

Occupation can be a method of intervention when it is sustained (see *Squatting*) or it can be a method of protest when it is short-term and symbolic – as in the case of some 60 people who marked out a volley-ball field, set up a net and began a game on the Walmer Estate site earmarked for houses for House of Representative MPs.

The protesters, many carrying spades, declared the area Freedom Park before dispersing on the orders of police who said they were an illegal gathering. (*Cape Times*, 7.5.86)

■ DEFIANT MINERS MOVES WIVES INTO HOSTELS

MIGRANT mineworkers at several Anglo American Corporation-controlled coal mines in the Eastern Transvaal have confronted the migrant labour system head on: they have unilaterally moved their wives or girlfriends into the single-sex hostels.

The move – done in defiance of mine management – is the first such public action following the NUM's pledge at their recent annual conference to "take control" of the compounds and dismantle the migrant labour system.

It creates an acute dilemma for mine management, who have repeatedly stated their opposition to the single-sex compound system but have been accused by the union of dragging their feet in changing it.

The "occupation" of the Anglo American Collieries (Amcoal) hostels started last weekend at Landau, Bank, Kriel and Goedehoop Collieries in the Witbank-Middelburg area.

Attempts by senior officials from the Chamber of Mines and mine management to stop the occupation of the hostels have been unsuccessful.

Workers have ignored a circular sent to their wives from management warning them their presence constitutes trespass.

– Weekly Mail, 3.4.87

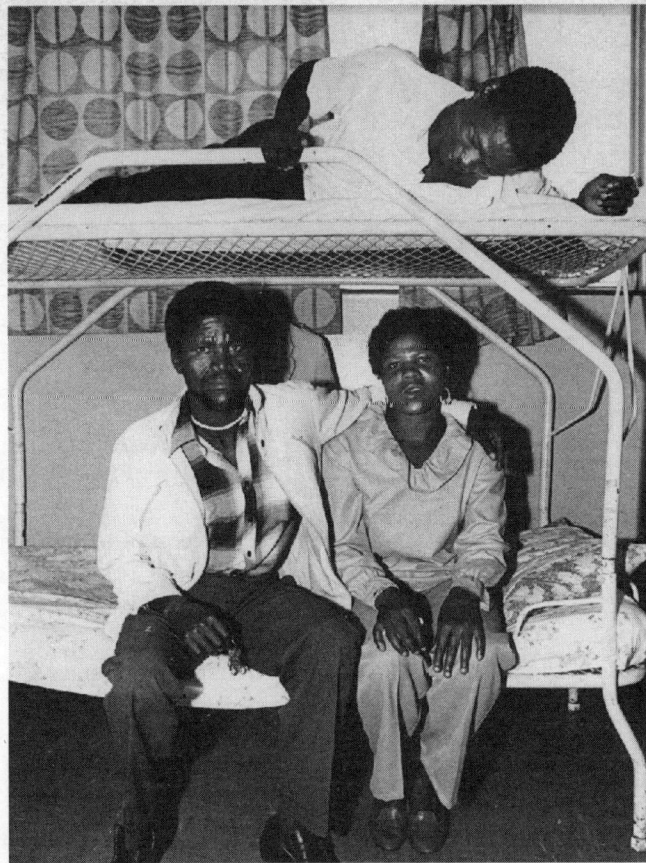

RIGHT
Witbank colliers in single sex hostels defy mine management in April 1987 by moving their wives in with them.

ERIC MILLER

OSTRACISM

Refusing to form or continue relations with a person or group can be a powerful form not only of non-cooperation, but of intervening against unacceptable behaviour. Ostracism can be practised against an opponent, as in the case of shopkeepers who refuse to deal with occupying troops during wartime. Its most extreme and effective application, however, is against a member or members of one's own group.

In SA, black members of the security forces and of official government structures have been treated like collaborators and have been forced to move from townships when ostracism degenerated into mob violence.

An individual who felt the sting of ostracism in 1989 was former *Sunday Times* journalist Jani Allen, who fled to London in the wake of the furore around her alleged association with right wing leader Eugene Terre'Blanche.

In an interview with *Fair Lady* (December 1989), Allen said: "I have been deeply affected by what has happened. From being the girl everyone wanted to know, I became a social embarrassment. People I thought were my friends disappeared faster than a bishop during a raid on a brothel. Overnight my mantelpiece, previously white with invitations, became a place for standing candlesticks."

Resistance heroine Winnie Mandela suffered formal rejection by her own community after events leading to the death of teenage activist Stompie Moeketsi. Among the factors leading to her gradual reintegration into anti-apartheid organisations was a perception, in the words of journalist Nomavenda Mathiane of *Frontline,* that it was unjust to "heap all the blame on one pair of shoulders, as if shunning her will solve the problems".

She writes: "All along there has been hypocrisy in the treatment of Winnie. I have known people who have appeared in newspapers hugging her, including whites, to privately tell all sorts of stories. Of the people who are rushing to distance themselves from her, some have for years known of courts and punishments behind her walls, and when her neighbours went to the leaders to tell of the screams, the leaders said it was the work of the struggle. Some prominent people have played the role of assistant judges."

■ WINNIE BANISHED – BY HER OWN PEOPLE

WINNIE Mandela has begun a term of banishment and internal exile in Soweto much harsher than her eight years of isolation in Brandfort.

This time it is not the Pretoria government, but her own people who have rejected her.

The reverberations of yesterday's unequivocal statement by the Mass Democratic Movement will take time to be felt around the world. Winnie Mandela has been excommunicated by the very struggle of which she had become a revered and potent symbol.

The statement, presented in Johannesburg yesterday by former UDF acting publicity secretary Murphy Morobe, UDF president Archie Gumede and Cosatu president Elijah Barayi, suggested that the substance – if not necessarily the details – of the allegations against her are true.

And news agency reports late yesterday said senior members of the ANC had been fully briefed on the issue and supported the efforts of the Soweto community. The ANC was in touch with those who were dealing with the crisis.

That the Johannesburg statement was issued with a deep sense of regret was clear throughout the press conference. It was "a very sensitive and painful matter," Morobe said.

He responded sharply when asked why it had taken so long for leaders to speak out on the Winnie Mandela issue: "Because it has not been an easy matter," he snapped. But, he added later: "History calls for a specific decision and we have taken it."

Mrs Mandela had "abused the trust and confidence which she had enjoyed over the years," the statement said, and she had failed to "consult the democratic movement, often violating the spirit and ethos of the movement".

While "paying tribute" to Mrs Mandela's contribution and acknowledging her suffering at the hands of the government and enforced separation from her husband, the representatives said "the stage has been reached where we have no option but to speak out".

The statement laid the blame for the conduct of the controversial "football team" squarely at Winnie's door. "In particular we are outraged by the reign of terror that the team has been associated with. Not only is Mrs Mandela associated with the team, in fact it is her own creation."

"We are outraged by Mrs Mandela's obvious complicity in the recent abductions (a reference to the four refugees forcibly removed from their sanctuary at

Orlando's Methodist Church). Had Stompie (Moeketsi) and his colleagues not been abducted by Mrs Mandela's 'football team', he would have been alive today."

The statement therefore "distanced the Mass Democratic Movement from Mrs Mandela and her actions", and "called on the people, in particular the Soweto community, to exercise this distancing in a dignified manner".

At the same time, it was repeatedly emphasised that the democratic movement "reaffirmed its unqualified support for our leader, Comrade Nelson Mandela, and called for his immediate release".

– Weekly Mail, 17.2.89

OVERLOADING

Deliberately increasing demands for services far beyond their capacity, so that the institution concerned is slowed down or paralysed, is a form of intervention. A government's administrative system may be overloaded through excessive compliance – giving unnecessary information, making many inquiries, being a nuisance. In Britain, where large numbers of people object to the presence of US Air Force bases, the telephone number of the US Embassy is often "blockaded" by large numbers of people ringing them up to convey protest messages.

■ ORDERLY, TALKATIVE AND PAINSTAKINGLY SLOW

PAMPHLETS giving details of how to disrupt First National Bank business throughout the country have been widely distributed on the Cape Flats.

The campaign against the bank is in retaliation for its decision to ignore the MDM's opposition to the presence of the World XV rugby team in SA.

"The MDM has through its various forums made known its opposition to the tour," says the pamphlet. "First National Bank has chosen to defy such opinion."

It continues: "The purpose is to fill the banking halls with so many people that other clients are unable to conduct their normal business. People should be orderly, but talkative and painstakingly slow."

The protesters who gathered outside the Adderley Street branch today said they had come to close their accounts at the bank.

The bank's doors were closed. Police told watching journalists to leave the area and cordoned off Adderley Street in front of the bank.

FNB manager Mr Eddie Kriel said later only one account at his branch – that of a trade union – had been closed because of the rugby tour.

– Weekend Argus, 26.8.89

■ THE EMERGENCY MADE SIMPLE

Should you intend discussing any of the following topics:
- Security force action
- Boycotts
- The treatment of detainees
- The release of any detainee
- People's courts
- Street committees

Simply phone these numbers to ask for permission:

P W Botha (021) 45-2225
Pik Botha (012) 28-6912
Chris Heunis (021) 45-7295
Magnus Malan (012) 26-6718
Adriaan Vlok (012) 323-8880
Kobie Coetsee (012) 323-8581
Stoffel Botha (012) 26-8081
Gerrit Viljoen (012) 28-5171
Barend du Plessis (012) 26-0261
Danie Steyn (012) 26-6568
Willie van der Merwe (012) 28-4773
Bureau for Information (012) 21-7397; (012) 21-7529; (012) 21-7396;
(012) 21-7528
Neil Barnard (012) 323-9761
P W van der Westhuizen (012) 325-4780

Section 3 (4)(a)(i) of yesterday's new emergency regulations authorises any minister, deputy minister or government official to allow discussion of these forbidden topics.

– Weekly Mail, 12.12.86

PETITION

Petitions may be signed by large numbers of individuals, or by a number of people representing organisations, institutions and constituencies. They have a long history, going back at least as far as the Roman Empire.

■ 250 000 SIGN ST LUCIA CAMPAIGN

JOHANNESBURG. – Another 100 000 signatures to save St Lucia from being mined for titanium have been sent to the Minister of Environmental Affairs, Mr Gert Kotzé – but he has already announced that he will not oppose mining.

Yesterday the environmental campaign, CARE, organised by *The Star* newspaper, delivered the signatures and the petition is now closed.

The petition, which began in September, became the biggest, by far, on any issue in SA's history.

The Star (with the help of the Wildlife Society and other bodies) collected 217 728 signatures and the *Natal Mercury* 60 420, bringing the counted total to 278 148.

But many thousands more were sent directly to the minister and to the state president.

Many hundreds of letters were received from groups at universities, technikons, businesses and individuals.

Last week Mr Kotze announced that, subject to a favourable environmental impact report, mining would be allowed to go ahead.

Environmental scientists have warned that the operation will certainly affect the ecosystem of Lake St Lucia.

– The Argus, 5.12.89

PICKETING

Historically the picket line has been the device of trade unions, developed to keep workers out of a struck factory. The aim is both to persuade and shame "scabs" into supporting the strike. A picket may also be a way of informing the public about a strike and the issues at stake.

Picketing is used more widely. For instance, shops selling boycotted goods have been picketed, as have law courts, corporate headquarters, government offices and parliaments.

An example of a very long and large picket is the Women's Peace Camp at Greenham Common, where the US Air Force maintains a Cruise missile base. The peace camp was set up in 1981 and still exists.

In countries where civil liberties are observed, pickets are often deployed outside embassies and consulates to protest against the policies of the governments concerned.

In SA, pickets have generally faced swift arrest.

RIGHT
Black Sash members hold a placard demonstration outside Parliament in Cape Town.

Courtesy of THE ARGUS

PLACARD DEMOS

The Black Sash is particularly well known for its tradition of staging placard demonstrations on busy roads during rush-hour, although many other organisations have used this method to raise awareness.

A legal placard demonstration is designed to comply with relevant laws and municipal by-laws which vary from place to place. In Pietermaritzburg, for instance, group stands have been permitted while in other centres stands have had to be individual to be legal.

POLL

Where the official electoral system prevents the opposition from participating fully or at all, a popular poll or mock election can be a useful and dramatic form of protest.

A full-scale mock election may be held or people may be asked to vote on a particular issue. Special polling places at which to vote may be set up, a postal vote may be organised, or people may be canvassed in the street and from door to door.

The poll run by the *Sowetan* newspaper in May 1987 resulted in posters displayed on street corners announcing "Nelson Mandela wins the vote".

PORTRAITS

Public display of the pictures of resistance heroes or others who symbolise the aims of the movement is sometimes used to communicate and strengthen political loyalties.

When ANC leader Govan Mbeki was released from jail in October 1987, bumper stickers and posters bearing his portrait were stuck up across the country. Marchers in the Western Cape calling for the release of Nelson Mandela in August 1985 carried his portrait with them.

It was illegal to publish a photograph of Nelson Mandela while he was imprisoned. When *Vrye Weekblad* and the *Weekly Mail* published an artist's impression in July 1989, his face had not been seen in public for a quarter of a century, as *Vrye Weekblad* put it.

■ THIS IS NELSON MANDELA TODAY

EVERYONE knows his name and how he looked more than 20 years ago when he was last photographed – but only a handful of people know what the world's most famous prisoner-turned-diplomat looks like today.

A Dutch artist has solved the problem, by spending many hours with people who have recently seen the ANC leader and constructing a life-like drawing. Nelson Mandela's associates have confirmed its realism, save that his hair is greyer and the lines around his mouth less pronounced than in the drawing.

– Weekly Mail, 14.7.89

PRAYER

The power of prayer or meditation in strengthening and transforming individuals is generally acknowledged but prayer can also function as a force for political and social transformation. The controversy that erupted after the SACC's "Call to Prayer for an End to Unjust Rule" on June 16 1986 highlighted the political power of prayer. That prayer and social action are linked is a notion central to liberation theology, which sees the mystical and the contemplative as the wellspring of creative NVA.

When key military leaders defected during the last days of the Marcos regime in the Philippines, Cardinal Jaime Sin went to three orders of enclosed nuns and told them: "We are now in battle. Prostrate yourselves, pray and fast. You are the powerhouse of God and central to the battle. Fast until death if necessary," Walter Wink recounts in *Jesus' Third Way*. The cardinal's next decisive step was to issue a call on the Catholic radio station requesting the people to interpose themselves between the defectors and government troops (see *Zabalaza*), which led to a nonviolent victory.

■ "O, Lord! Despite a great many prayers to You we are continually losing our wars. Tomorrow we shall again be fighting a battle that is truly great. With all our might we need Your help and that is why I must tell You something. This battle tomorrow is going to be a serious affair. There will be no place in it for children. Therefore I must ask You not to send Your Son to help us. Come Yourself."

– Prayer of Koq, leader of the Griquas, before a battle with Afrikaners in 1876.
Quoted in *Another Day of Life by Rysard Kapuscinski, Picador, 1988*

■ INTER-FAITH SERVICE PRAYS FOR NEW ORDER

ABOUT 250 people packed the St John's chapel in St George's Cathedral last night when a brief inter-faith service was held at the start of an 18-hour vigil.

Those present had come to "reject apartheid, pray for a new and just order, and show solidarity with the oppressed," said Mrs Jenny de Tolly, a member of the Black Sash and Votes for All Alliance, organisers of the vigil, which ends at 2pm today with another service.

Last night's brief service took place under the glare of television lights and the click of cameras.

The Rev Syd Luckett conducted the service, which included a poem by Pablo Neruda and a reading from a Nicaraguan priest.

Rabbi Myer Benjamin read a meditational poem and a Jewish service was then held just outside the entrance to the cathedral. Such services may not be held within a place of worship of another religion.

Rabbi Benjamin lit the traditional light of remembrance "for the dead and detained".

Proceedings continued with statements from various of the 13 organisations in the Votes for All Alliance.

– *Cape Times, 6.5.87*

PROGRAMMES

Programmes differ from short-term campaigns by emphasising the long-term structures and modes of behaviour desired for the future, instead of what stands in their way. Gandhi insisted that freedom from British rule was only the beginning of real independence for India. As important was rebuilding the self-sufficiency of the villages, where 80% of the population lived in poverty, and this was the aim of Gandhi's "constructive programme".

Programme workers participated in village life, taking part in the menial work necessary to implement health measures such as sanitation. Like Gandhi, they spun and wove cloth, wearing hand-woven clothes. For the spinning wheel at which Gandhi worked daily was not a fad, but a symbol of the revival of cottage industries that he hoped would spur the economic regeneration of rural India.

The late Lanza del Vasto, leader of the NV movement in France until his death in 1981, shared Gandhi's mistrust of Western "development" strategies and technology.

"In those Third World countries attempting mechanisation and rapid industrial growth – like Brazil and India – there is immense repression and increased suffering," he said.

"Gandhi found a better way: dig wells, develop agriculture, stay on the land. If you are very numerous, avoid machines – they put people out of work."

Rural poverty is only one problem area that constructive programmes must address. Urban housing, education and health are others.

The recent growth in SA of "people's education" – even if largely in future-oriented planning rather than implementation – is a hopeful example of this form of NVA. Methodology, courses of study and resource books are being investigated and compiled. The NECC's *What is History?* (1987) and the Association of Law Societies of SA's *Street Law* (1987) are examples.

PUBLISHING

The old maxim that the pen is mightier than the sword found special application in SA when the crusading young weekly, *Vrye Weekblad*, published the confessions of self-confessed death squad leader Dirk Coetzee, and helped to hasten the end of an official reign of terror.

Vrye Weekblad is one of a crop of new publications that were born out of a

103

need to nurture and reflect an emergent political culture in print while the established media continued to mirror the old order.

Collectively known as the alternative press, these publications – *Weekly Mail, Vrye Weekblad, New Nation, South, Grassroots, Die Suid-Afrikaan, Work in Progress, Saamstaan,* etc – had both the courage and the flexibility, thanks to funding and small circulations that reduced financial risk, to fly in the face of emergency media restrictions. They suffered the consequences in the form of bannings, suspensions and warnings as the SA government continuously refined its methods of censorship.

■ MOLO'S CHARMS OVERCOME PROBLEMS

MOLO Songololo (Xhosa for "good morning, Centipede") first began crawling in 1979, the International Year of the Child. Founder members Nomhi Tulumane and Nomphle Kelelo started a research project with a group of Std 4 and 5 children in Crossroads. They asked children to draw and write about their personal history and experiences in the township.

The wealth of material collected was to be published in book form by Ravan, but many felt this would be too expensive a buy for most children.

A strong argument was made for a magazine project to reflect the ideas, feelings and experiences of children in a more effective way. In March 1980, 2 000 copies were printed.

To give children an idea of what the magazine was about, they were asked to write about "the biggest problem in SA". This attracted a tremendous response, varying from "the problem is shacks are leaking when it is raining and very hot when it is hot", to "the big problem is mice an crakes an merds and guns and seas an snak's an sinking sand", and "the group area where people put you where they want to ... a letter comes and says that you must move. These hurt the people. My idea is that everyone must fight back."

Molo had bad teething problems. Teachers and principals did not want the magazine in the schools for fear of the education department. But Molo's charms, and its invaluable service to both teachers and pupils, eventually overcame the problems.

Today Molo distributes 15 000 magazines to more than 200 schools. Language barriers are broken by stories in English, Afrikaans and Xhosa. Historical content is presented through the lives of national heroes like Biko and Mandela in a fun story form.

– South, 15.4.87

See also: Information, Underground

QUESTIONING

Opposition to a system often begins with questions in individual consciences. To organise around such questions, and to ask them publicly, is not to "provoke opposition" but to reflect it, as War Resistance Movement activist Laurie Nathan told a workshop on alternative national service in November 1989.

"Initially conscripts began asking what they were fighting for and who they were fighting against when the SADF started to play a more coercive role. There was the invasion of Angola in 1975, the mobilisation of the SADF during the Soweto uprising, and the start of the full-scale border war in Namibia.

"The organised WRM took root in the late 1970s when conscientious objectors were imprisoned and English-language churches took a stand on the rights of conscientious objectors.

"The most critical phase of growth in the history of the movement was in the mid-1980s and was a direct response to the SADF's involvement in the townships, with the deployment of literally thousands of troops – according to the Minister of Defence it was up to 35 000 troops – in black townships throughout the country. That was the point at which conscription became an issue of concern not merely to a small number of highly politicised people, but to the white community in general.

"In the late 1980s after the SADF's extensive involvement in Angola, we found through informal sources that there was a significant increase in the number of men failing to report for army camps. At the same time there was a significant increase in support for the ECC. There was also an unprecedented wave of opposition from the mainstream Afrikaans-speaking community. The NGK's official publication *Die Kerkbode* issued a critical editorial questioning – not on pragmatic grounds, but on moral and ethical grounds – whether the SADF involvement in Angola was justified.

"The Minister of Defence responded on SATV with a scathing attack on the editorial. NGK moderator Johan Heyns responded the next day with some words that I think capture the essence of the WRM: 'These questions that were asked in the editorial are legitimate. These are the questions that are in the hearts of our people.' "

QUESTIONNAIRE

Surveys are sometimes used to manipulate issues, but questionnaires can be used by communities to establish common needs and goals and to back representations to authorities with evidence of widespread concern.

"Last October Philip van Niekerk reported in a front-page article in *Weekly Mail:* 'A major nation-wide survey released yesterday has revealed that two thirds of black South Africans support sanctions.' But in an article in the same newspaper Steve Friedman offered a different view. He drew attention to the 60% who were opposed to sanctions if they increased unemployment, seeing it as a counterpoint to the two-thirds who support either unconditional or conditional sanctions as a means of ending apartheid. Friedman reckoned: 'Politicians and academics tend to use surveys of black opinion in much the same way as Humpty Dumpty used words – they mean what they want them to mean'..." (Patrick Laurence, *Leadership* 1988/89)

■ COMMUNITY THAT LOOKED INTO ITS OWN HEART

MANENBERG. The name of a haunting melody, made famous by jazz pianist Abdullah Ebrahim. Also the name of the township he lived in, rather less well known than the song.

But that could change now. The township behind the song has taken the initiative to launch a pioneering survey in which residents look into their own hearts.

The Manenberg Ministers Fraternal, an interdenominational body of clergymen, decided recently to do something about the township's many problems, including poverty, homelessness and crime.

They began discussions with local community organisations, and together came up with the idea of a centre sited in the heart of Manenberg's flatland, offering advice and counselling to individuals, and a place where groups could explore ways of tackling their problems.

But what did the people of Manenberg themselves want the centre to be? It was decided there was only one way to find out: by carrying out a survey. But it was not to be an ordinary survey.

Heather Petersen, co-ordinator of the Manenberg research group, explains: "The community was involved in every stage of the process and residents carried out the actual survey themselves."

The research collective – made up of academics from the universities of Cape Town and the Western Cape and the Organisation for Appropriate Social Services in SA – ran a series of workshops aimed not only at training interviewers but also in determining the shape of the survey itself.

"There was initially a great deal of suspicion, although we had a clear mandate to do the research," Petersen says.

"Researchers usually go into a community, ask questions, raise expectations and then are never seen again. They get their PhD or write a book, and the people are left with their problems. We agreed no one would get a degree out of the research, no students would be used and residents would do the survey themselves.

"We'd stopped and renegotiated the research design. We workshopped how the questionnaire should look, what should be asked, how to word it so it would be accessible. "In a series of what came to be known as "die rooi pamflette", the community was informed about the survey and later its findings.

"The survey has proved invaluable as a voice of the people of Manenberg," said Petersen. "The information will be used to build a centre that will address people's real concerns, rather than those postulated by social scientists and welfare workers. It won't be seen as something imposed on the community. The need for it was defined by the people."

– *Weekly Mail, 7.7.89*

QUITTING

The resignation of Dr Van Zyl Slabbert as leader of the PFP, the official opposition, and as an MP on February 7 1986 brought home a point the white SA electorate did not wish to hear when it voted on the tricameral parliament in the referendum of 1983: that the black majority could not be excluded from a new constitutional dispensation.

RIGHT
Dr F Van Zyl Slabbert leaves parliament for the last time as official leader of the Opposition after quitting in February 1986.

Courtesy of THE ARGUS

He said parliament's reaction to the events of 1985 – when the country was engulfed by violence – had been "a grotesque exercise in irrelevancy". At the end of the week-long no-confidence debate he had been left with "an overwhelming feeling of absurdity".

In a 1987 speech titled "The Relevance of Parliament" which became his major statement on the subject of his resignation, he noted that his objections were to "the present parliament in the present time", and not objections in principle. The present parliament did not provide for representative government; had transfered its sovereignty and accountability to an excecutive president; and specifically made it "constitutionally impossible for the majority of the adult population to change the government of the day peacefully".

Other high-profile resignations represented the haemorrhaging of the ruling establishment itself. Mr Wynand Malan left the National Party but retained the Randburg seat as an independent in the general election of 1987 and later formed the National Democratic Movement (NDM), and Dr Denis Worrall resigned as SA Ambassador to the UK and returned to SA to contest Helderberg, the seat then held by Minister of Constitutional Development and Planning Chris Heunis. Worrall founded the Independent Party which, with Malan's NDM and the PFP, combined to form the Democratic Party. Other defectors who helped found the DP included Nasionale Pers board member and ex-MD David de Villiers, *Rapport* editor Willem de Klerk and Stellenbosch economics professor Sampie Terreblanche, who shook the establishment again when he quit the Broederbond in 1989.

The period leading up to the 1989 elections saw a tactical reassessment of changing white parliamentary politics on the part of the ANC, which declared it would not oppose participation in the House of Assembly elections, and the MDM, which after intense debate declared a neutral position, one step away from the previous position of the UDF, which had been born in response to the constitutional exclusion of blacks and had advocated a complete boycott of the previous general elections.

■ CROSSROADS: URBAN FOUNDATION QUITS

THE Urban Foundation has withdrawn its stewardship of Operation Upgrade Crossroads – claiming government policy on the squatter town "legitimises violence as a method of achieving community objectives".

The UF said the government had set a "dangerous precedent" in not allowing the over 30 000 refugees from last week's violence to return to their home sites.

Many refugees would not accept the government's sole option of moving to Khayelitsha. This raised the "strong possibility of forced removals and the further spreading of violence rather than containing it," UF regional director Colin Appleton said.

– *City Press, 1.6.86*

■ ENTIRE VILLAGE COUNCIL RESIGNS

PORT ELIZABETH. – Cradock's Lingelihle Village Council – one of the first 29 community councils to become a fully-fledged council under the Black Local Authorities Act last year – resigned en masse last week.

Councillors said they had abdicated because the community regarded them as civil servants who assisted the government in implementing apartheid.

In addition, the council had been unable to improve conditions in the township because they were not given a hearing by the authorities.

– *Cape Times, 7.1.85*

RADIO

Radio broadcasts beamed to occupied countries during World War II were an important means of informing people, boosting the morale of those resisting the Nazis, and passing coded messages to resistance agents.

When the Soviets invaded Czechoslovakia in 1968, clandestine radio broadcasts kept the Czechs informed and declared opposition to the invasion for up to two weeks after it began.

In pre-1990 SA, phone-in programmes provided an opportunity to express moderate opinions, and musical request programmes were used to greet friends in hiding, while independent stations like 702 offered livelier political interviews than the SABC; but state control left room for little else.

■ THEIR RADIO'S SILENT, BUT STUDENT BROADCASTERS ARE NOT

UNIVERSITY of Cape Town campus radio plans to challenge the Geneva-based International Telecommunications Union over the recent sealing off of their transmitters by post office officials.

While they realise their placing of home-made FM transmitters in five university residences was illegal, UCT Radio staffers believe the action should be seen in the context of the state's attack on the media.

Station director Ian Koenigsfest and news director Alan Davidson said they were writing to the ITU "which is responsible for handing out airwaves internationally", challenging "the fact that the SABC controls the airwaves rather than regulating them".

"Our fundamental demand is that legitimate alternative radio stations should be given the right to apply for broadcasting licences. We find it quite absurd that no channels exist for licence application, regardless of how limited the signal is," said Koenigsfest.

UCT Radio sees the radio legislation as serving the same function as the silencing of the press. "Ultimately we are the losers as the culture of silence descends on us."

– Weekly Mail, 13.5.88

RAID

A nonviolent raid usually involves a march on a place of symbolic importance, culminating in a demand for possession of the area. In some cases, large numbers of people may surround "seized" points so that officials can't get back into them. This type of action carries a heavy risk of severe countermeasures by police and troops.

Perhaps the most famous nonviolent raid ever undertaken was that on the Dharasana Salt Works of the British Raj, some 300km north of Bombay, on May 21 1930.

The raid followed Gandhi's arrest, after his 200-mile march to the sea to make illegal salt had aroused resistance across India. It was conducted by over 2 500 volunteers of the Indian National Congress, led by Mrs Sarojini Naidu.

What happened was recorded by Web Miller of United Press in a dispatch published in over 1 000 newspapers in India and abroad:

"In complete silence the Gandhi men drew up and halted 100 yards from the stockade. A picked column advanced from the crowd, waded the dikes and approached the barbed wire stockade.

"Suddenly scores of policemen rushed on the advancing marchers and rained down blows on their heads with their steel-shod lathis. Not one of the marchers even raised an arm to fend off the blows. They went down like ten-pins.

"From where I stood I heard the sickening whack of clubs on unprotected skulls. The waiting crowd of marchers groaned and sucked in their breath in sharp pain at every blow.

"The survivors, without breaking ranks, silently and doggedly marched on until struck down."

Two of the marchers were killed and 320 seriously wounded. Many were kicked in the stomach and testicles after they fell to the ground. Many were dragged to the ditches around the factory and thrown in. Mrs Naidu was among those arrested.

But the violence of the British police, sharply exposed by the courageous nonviolence of its victims, aroused widespread revulsion – even in England. The Viceroy was shaken by the unexpected strength of the Congress campaign and pride was kindled up and down India.

Just over a year later, the Viceroy met Gandhi and agreed that jailed protesters would be released and Indians would be allowed to make salt. In return Gandhi suspended the civil disobedience campaign. (Based on material from Kumar and Puri: *Mahatma Gandhi, His Life and Influence,* Heinemann, London, 1982.)

■ SHOPPERS IN CLOVER 'TROLLEY PROTEST'

SUPPORTERS of the 168 workers dismissed last year from Clover dairies' Pietermaritzburg plant visited supermarkets throughout Durban on New Year's Eve and filled shopping trolleys with Clover, Sacca, Elite and NCD products.

The products, which were dumped at various points in the supermarkets, were replaced by pamphlets highlighting the plight of the dismissed workers.

Similar action was undertaken by sympathetic shoppers during the Cape red meat boycott a few years ago.

Nearly six months have passed since the dismissals, but the bosses have refused to reinstate workers.

The company's intransigence has met with a nationwide consumer boycott of Clover products as well as products manufactured by National Co-operative dairies (NCD) and its subsidiaries.

– New Nation, 8.1.87

See also: Wading in

RALLIES

In SA, gatherings have been banned at various times since the early 1950s. All open-air gatherings except sports meetings were banned after 1983. Indoor meetings dealing with school boycotts were banned in March 1985, as were meetings dealing with stayaways in 16 districts in the Eastern Cape and two in the Transvaal. Specific meetings or meetings of particular organisations, ranging from the UDF to local PTSAs, were often banned or prevented.

In the wake of the release of the "Sisulu Seven", FW de Klerk's administration relaxed restrictions to allow an ANC Welcome Home Rally. The rally was used as a platform for peace and represented a triumph for discipline. But it demonstrated that the ANC had been catapulted into a new set of political circumstances in which it would have to rethink the nonviolent arm of its strategies, and that rallies present a challenge to their organisers as well as to their opponents.

Contrasting the ANC leaders with the SACP, which "retains a romantic mystique" even in the more open political climate, the *Weekly Mail* pointed to the demythologising properties of public political activity.

"The legendary leaders . . . are dignified and solid, but at the same time they are human beings capable of delivering boring speeches..."

■ ANC: FROM SYMBOLS TO POLITICIANS

THE Soccer City rally showed what many commentators knew already – that, despite its exclusion from legal politics for nearly 30 years (partly because of it?), the ANC can rely on a substantial support base, probably a bigger one than any other movement.

Rallies of this size are, of course, unique by SA standards: the ANC veterans never addressed meetings this large during the movement's heyday as a legal organisation. It obviously needed organisation to ensure that the meeting happened without incident.

The organisers managed to show that a mass rally in support of the ANC can be an entirely normal event: it will now be harder for the white establishment to resist demands for the freeing of political activity.

But if the 65 000 – 70 000 people who attended were more than any other group could have drawn, they were still not enough to fill a single football stadium.

. . . Few people attend political rallies spontaneously – particularly people who, like black South Africans, are not used to expressing their political allegiances openly.

Attendance has to be organised – any movement which simply calls a meeting and assumes that its potential supporters will arrive is likely to be disappointed.

People are also far more likely to attend if they are already members of an organised movement: most people in the stadium were there as members of organised worker, student or civic groups.

In other words, attendance at rallies may be a test of a movement's organisation rather than its support. The size of the crowd may show that, while the ANC's mass organisation has made strides in the past few years, it has some way to go . . . .

Apartheid policies have never been more vulnerable than they are now and organised mass campaigns against residential, health and education apartheid are more likely to win gains than in the past. So too are campaigns by township residents for more power over the decisions which affect them.

In the present climate, these campaigns may allow mass movements to build the power base they need. Far from being a substitute for their fight to win power in central government, they may be the only way of getting there.

– Steven Friedman, *Weekly Mail, 3.11.89*

RECORDING

A remarkable recording project was undertaken secretly by the Catholic Church in Brazil in the 1970s, when military repression and institutionalised torture seemed unstoppable. It had four parts:

1. Collecting an archive of the official records of proceedings in the military courts between 1964 and 1979.

2. Establishing a library of some 5 000 publications issued by clandestine human rights groups.

3. Analysing the data in a 7 000-page study which included 111 statistical tables and an alphabetical list of 444 torturers whose names were taken from official military records.

4. Publishing a book, *Brazil: Never Again*, which summarised the results of the project and sold more copies than any other non-fiction work in the history of Brazil. (*One World*, June 1986)

There is a saying in Mozambique – "Our old people are our libraries." This insight is one of many that is inspiring oral history projects in SA in an attempt to put a one-sided record straight.

■ NONVIOLENT OPTION ATTEMPT FOR SA

PORT ELIZABETH. – A new organisation, launched in PE at the beginning of this month, will attempt to create "a nonviolent option for SA".

The executive director of Operation Real SA, Mr Rory Riordan, said yesterday opinions from people within and without the townships about the objectives of the organisation had been "tremendously positive".

It is an organisation that will cater only for the Eastern Cape, with the objectives to monitor, intervene in and record the political situation – particularly within the townships.

Projects would include the recording of the real SA situation by creating a data bank of documents that would "truly and graphically tell the story of SA as it is".

Information for this purpose would be obtained from newspapers and journals, court records and judgments, statements, affidavits and notes taken by reliable sources.

– Cape Times, 11.10.86

REFUSING RECOGNITION

Opponents of a government or institution may refuse to co-operate with its agencies, departments and structures, thus showing that they do not recognise it.

■ THE WOMAN WHO WOULD NOT CARRY A PASS

A VETERAN women's rights activist died in New Brighton last Saturday night without ever having carried a pass, a reference book or an identity document.

Pauline Nombayiso Mbunye, 74, a founder and executive member of the Port Elizabeth Women's Organisation, died of natural causes at a friend's home.

Her refusal to carry an identity document disqualified her from housing, a formal job, and, eventually, a pension.

Friends say she stopped wearing shoes when Nelson Mandela was imprisoned. She told them this made her more determined than ever never to carry a pass. Thus, she told friends, she would never have a job – and could not afford to become accustomed to wearing shoes.

– Weekly Mail, 7.8.87

RENOUNCING

Refusing to accept or renouncing honour or rank may be a way of registering protest against the government or institution conferring it. Poet and Nobel Prize winner Rabindranath Tagore, a friend and admirer of Gandhi, renounced the knighthood conferred on him by the British in protest against the Amritsar massacre of April 1919 in which some 400 people, including women and children, were shot dead by British troops under the command of General Dyer.

■ A ROOM FULL OF MEN IN DRESSES, DEBATING THE RIGHTS OF WOMEN

A ROOM full of men wearing ankle-length dresses in a range of colours, all with intricate buttoning detail, inverted pleats and sashes, some with ruffles at the wrist and flashy jewellery, solemnly debated whether women were by nature qualified to join them.

To be fair, the Anglican synod, meeting in Durban for the last nine days, also included a number of laymen and women – and a majority voted in favour of ordaining women to the priesthood.

The issue was debated for virtually a whole day, at the end of which 121 voted in favour and 79 against – 13 votes short of the two-thirds majority needed to change church law on the subject.

A number of the clergy have protested against the decision.

Archbishop Desmond Tutu's personal chaplain, Chris Ahrends, has requested that he be allowed to step down as a priest. He said this was a symbolic gesture of solidarity with women. If Tutu grants his request Ahrends will revert to the status of deacon – an order to which women are admitted.

Subsequently another priest, theology lecturer Torquil Paterson, stood up to speak at the synod and was called to order because he was wearing a suit and tie instead of priest's robe.

He said he had chosen not to wear a cassock to indicate his support for women who were not allowed to wear the robe.

– Weekly Mail, 9.6.89

RESISTING REMOVAL

Among the many examples of this method of non-cooperation, undertaken by thousands of South Africans, is the battle fought by Actstop, formed early in 1979 to fight the eviction of Indian families from the (white) Johannesburg suburb of Pageview.

In the frontline was the Naidu family who decided to live on the pavement after being evicted. Neighbours provided a tent and local clergyman Rob Robertson and other sympathisers joined them at night.

After five weeks police confiscated the Naidu's tent and other belongings under the Prevention of Illegal Squatting Act. The family spent several more nights on the pavement without shelter until Robertson, as a white, rented the house they had been evicted from and invited them to stay with him as guests – something the law permitted for up to three months.

In this breathing space, Actstop was formed, court cases were fought and a petition addressed to the Minister of Community Development. Robertson and other volunteers hung posters saying "Spare this house, people need it" on habitable dwellings scheduled for demolition. As a result he was charged with malicious damage to property and fined R50.

Meanwhile, massive publicity had been instrumental in suspending evictions and they stopped altogether after a court ruling that the state could not evict people in terms of the Group Areas Act without providing alternative accommodation.

RIGHT
A meeting in the rural area of Mogopa to protest government plans for removal.

PAUL WEINBERG

AND NOW WE HAVE NO LAND – THE STRUGGLE OF THE MOGOPA PEOPLE

THE two adjoining Mogopa farms are situated in the Ventersdorp area. The farms were bought by the ancestors of the dispossessed Mogopa in 1912 and 1931 respectively. For decades the Mogopa people devoted themselves to farming and developing their community. By 1984 there were two schools, a clinic, numerous shops, a reservoir and a thriving farming sector. Cash crops were sold to the local co-operative.

From October 1981 it became apparent that the government had decided to remove the Mogopa people in the interests of grand apartheid. To this end the government worked together with the discredited headman, Jacob More. The tribe had accused More of various acts of corruption and wanted him deposed. The local commissioner responded to their request by stating: "I as a white man and magistrate of this whole area say Jacob More will rule until he dies."

In 1981 officials of the Department of Co-operation and Development announced that More had agreed to removal on behalf of the tribe. The Mogopa people vehemently rejected this plan. The community thought they were now safe. However, unbeknown to them, negotiations between Jacob More, his committee and the department continued.

The department's trucks arrived in June 1983 to begin the removal. Since very

115

few people knew of the "negotiations", only ten families left with Jacob More. The department then returned towards the end of June and knocked down the school and withdrew its staff. At the same time three churches and the medical clinic were destroyed. The bus service between Ventersdorp and Mogopa was stopped and the pumps which were used to pump water into the reservoir were removed. The government was hoping to demoralise the people and force them to leave "voluntarily". This tactic had some effect. By 21 August 1983, 170 families had left Mogopa and gone to Pachsdraai. However, over 350 families remained at Mogopa.

The remaining families issued a legal challenge to the presence of a bulldozer which knocked down houses of people who left the village for any reason. The government responded by withdrawing the bulldozer. However, it issued the tribe with a "Removal Order" stating that they must leave Mogopa within ten days or be forcibly removed. An interdict was sought to stop the implementation of the order. The interdict and leave to appeal was refused. The tribe then petitioned the chief justice for leave to appeal. When the tenth day of the removal order dawned, many people, including Bishop Tutu, Allan Boesak, members of the Black Sash and UDF attended a vigil at Mogopa so as to be there when the forced removal was to take place. However, after an inspection of the crowd, the contingent of government officials and police withdrew.

After the removal deadline passed the community rebuilt the school and managed to have the bus service and pensions payments restored. They were confident that they would remain at Mogopa forever. However, on February 14 1984, the department proceeded with the removal notwithstanding the fact that the petition for leave to appeal was before the Appeal Court.

The removal came without warning. The area was cordoned off, the phones were cut and the police moved in. In one day, the remaining 350 families were moved to Pachsdraai and in the process another independent black farming community was destroyed.

At Pachsdraai they were met by rows of tin toilets and the headman, Jacob More. All the facilities were given to More and his "planning committee" to allocate. They allocated themselves the houses that had belonged to the white farmers. The doors, windowframes and roofing materials from the smashed schools at Mogopa are now in the big shed in the deposed headman's yard. The allocation of all fields and grazing was also controlled by More and his committee.

The Mogopa refused to stay under these conditions and almost immediately left for Bethanie. It was felt that Bethanie would be an improvement as it is the home of the Mogopa people's paramount chief. However, conditions in Bethanie turned out to be appalling and have steadily worsened over the last three years.

By December 1986 the once proud and prosperous landowners had been reduced to ragged, destitute squatters. The desire to return to Mogopa became increasingly intense. The possibility of a solution occurred in December 1986 when the government agreed to meet representatives of the Mogopa people. However, they were offered an alternative piece of land, "Kaffirskraal". The alternative offered was, for a number of reasons, completely unacceptable to the community. Firstly, if the community settled there they would have to accept incorporation into Bophuthatswana. Secondly, they would merely be tenants on the land and have no security of tenure. Thirdly, President Mangope has stated that because the Mogopa people had defied him, he would ensure that ultimately they would end up in Pachsdraai. The community asked the government to reconsider these conditions but were met with a refusal. Thus they became even more resolved to return to Mogopa.

It was evident that the possibility of the government allowing the people to return to Mogopa was remote. Thus after many meetings between the Mogopa people and support groups such as the SACC and TRAC it was decided that Mogopa people would participate in a church project to buy land for dispossessed communities. This project was initiated by the Machavie people who were removed 16 years ago.

The Botshabelo Trust was established to buy Holgat, a large farm in the Ventersdorp area. Close on R3m was raised to buy the farm from the Hermannsburg Mission of the Lutheran Church. Legal opinion had ascertained that even in the context of apartheid, black settlement at Holgat was perfectly legal. This was because as an old mission the Holgat farm is "released land" in terms of the 1913 Land Act. Numerous meetings were held with the Mogopa and Machavie communities to discuss the project. Studies were done to ascertain its feasibility.

By the beginning of July all the loose ends had been tied and there was a great sense of anticipation and excitement. The first instalment had been paid and the only aspect that remained was the official registration of the transfer of ownership. This was expected to occur in mid-July.

The transfer of ownership never took place. On July 7 the government expropriated Holgat.

– Black Sash newsletter, 3.8.87

IN September 1987 Mogopa's people, exasperated by their long diaspora, threatened a defiant march back to their land. This was called off after the government undertook to guarantee that future sites for the community would be held in freehold and would not be incorporated into any "homeland".

A meeting between Development Aid Minister Gerrit Viljoen and the community is due to take place at the end of the month where the minister is likely to make a final offer of alternative land. It is expected the community will urge him to reconsider their offer to buy back the farm they call their "fatherland".

. . . During negotiations Viljoen has turned down a bid by the Botshabelo Trust to buy the land back. "The proposal," said the minister, "cannot be considered favourably in view of the cabinet's decision that the (people of) Mogopa may not return to these farms."

. . . The farm is in the middle of a district dominated by the Conservative Party.

Some 4 000 people were expelled by force from Mogopa on February 14 1983 and the land leased to local white farming unions. One of the farmers who now grazes his cattle on the land is said to be the brother of Afrikaner Weerstandsbeweging leader Eugene Terre'Blanche.

– Weekly Mail, 17.2.89

SACRIFICE

The principle of sacrifice underlies the nonviolent philosophy. Sacrifices may be relatively small – like giving up luxuries; they may be substantial – like the three days' wages lost by two to three-million workers during the June 1988 Days of Protest; they may be enormous, involving the almost certain loss of freedom, and, in extreme circumstances, loss of life.

Sacrifice as a particular method of NVA means taking discomfort, humiliation, penalties or suffering upon oneself. It may involve giving away one's property, destroying one's shelter, exposing one's body to the elements.

Gandhi said: "Man lives freely by his readiness to die, if need be at the hand of his brother, never by killing him. Just as one must learn the art of killing in the training for violence, so one must learn the art of dying in the training for nonviolence. The votary of nonviolence has to cultivate the capacity for sacrifice of the highest order to be free from fear."

After being stripped of his chieftainship by the government for taking part in the 1952 Defiance Campaign, Chief Albert Luthuli said: "It is inevitable that in working for freedom some individuals and some families must take the lead and suffer: the road to freedom is via the cross." (Karis & Carter: *From Protest to Challenge*, Vol II, Hoover Institution Press, Stanford, California, 1987)

■ PEASANT REVOLT LED BY A MODERN LEAR

FOR more than two weeks, 100 000 peasants have laid siege to the Commissioner's office in Meerut, 50 miles from Delhi, in what has become a demonstration without parallel in independent India.

The farmers are led by Mahendra Singh Tikait, a 63-year-old cane-growing upper-caste Sikh. Until a year ago he was unknown outside the 84 villages of Uttar Pradesh, of which he is chieftain; now the whole country knows him.

He sits in a dusty open field outside the Commissioner's office, on a makeshift wooden platform as exposed to the elements as anything King Lear would have chosen to use. (Of the protest's seven martyrs, six have died of cold and one of a tractor accident.)

Tikait's supporters are small farmers – peasants with a land-holding of anything from half an acre to six. They say they want a 25 percent increase in sugar-cane prices, a 20 percent drop in fertilizer costs and a waiver of the past year's electricity bills and land taxes.

The farmers, Tikait says, will not budge until their demands are met. "For 40 years the city has exploited the farm. It's got to stop."

Girilal Jain, editor of the *Times of India,* wrote: "The sight of a few hundred thousand peasants sitting quietly day after day in an open ground and thousands of volunteers bringing food for them from neighbouring villages and distributing it in an orderly fashion must amaze anyone who is familiar with the behaviour of Indian crowds. The whole exercise has been breathtaking."

– Observer, 14.2.88

SANCTIONS

International debate about imposing sanctions and other forms of economic non-cooperation on SA intensified after the declaration of a nationwide state of emergency on June 12 1986 – although limited sanctions were already in force. These included a US package imposed by order of President Ronald Reagan in September 1985, Commonwealth measures agreed on at the Bahamas summit in October 1985, an EEC package adopted in Brussels in September 1985, and the UN arms embargo.

In 1986, SA's major trading partners – the US, UK and West Germany – were continuing to resist pressure to impose further sanctions. But the Commonwealth drew up restrictive measures, international bankers refused to roll over loans and, on September 29 1986, the US House of Representatives voted 313 to 83 – well over the two-thirds majority required to override a presidential veto – to enact a comprehensive sanctions bill.

Among its main provisions were a ban on new US loans and investments in SA, a ban on importing SA uranium, coal and textiles, a withdrawal of US landing rights for SA Airways and a ban on US flights to SA. Previous bans on exports to SA of crude oil, petroleum products, arms or equipment associated with nuclear power were reaffirmed.

In November 1989, the Washington-based International Freedom Foundation reported it was unlikely that President Bush would veto further sanctions if Congress passed them in 1990. In December 1989 *The Argus* reported that "the very best SA could hope for next year is a stricter enforcement of the 1986 Comprehensive Anti-Apartheid Act".

While it was clear that the trend was for the imposition of increasingly severe sanctions on SA, it was not clear how effective they were – the Comprehensive Anti-apartheid Act (CAAA) affected only a small percentage of exports – and it was equally unclear that the intent to apply pressure was greater than the self-interest which had been responsible for weakening existing measures. For instance, in September 1987 Norway ended all trade with SA – with one crucial exception: regulations preventing crude oil shipments to SA in Norwegian tankers excepted cargoes whose final destination was decided at sea.

Another example was SA coal, excluded from sanctions packages by both the EEC and Japan, which bought 20% or $1 430m of SA's coal exports in 1986.

Japan imposed sanctions on SA in September 1986 (steel and iron imports banned, travel to SA restricted, direct investment banned, new bank loans banned, military and computer sales to government institutions banned), but figures released in October 1987 showed that Japan's trade with SA had increased 25% during 1986, to a value of some $3 600m.

And in December 1987, the UN Security Council expressed "alarm and great concern that large quantities of military equipment were still reaching SA directly or via clandestine routes". Chile and Israel were reported by the Norway-based World Campaign against Military and Nuclear Collaboration with SA to be primarily responsible. An international arms fair in Santiago, Chile, in March 1988 included an exhibition of Armscor weaponry. *(Keesing's Contemporary Archives,* Vol XXXII, September 1986, XXXIV, January 1988 and XXXIV, October 1988; *Cape Times,* 5.8.88; *The Argus,* 4.5.88; *City Press,* 10.8.86.)

Disinvestment proved even more problematic. Buy-back clauses, franchise warehousing and licensing agreements do not constitute non-cooperation. And white SA, so far from being squeezed, was "happily snapping up everything on offer. In a single week, Anglo American managed to take over Ford's share of Samcor and also the local subsidiary of America's largest bank, Citicorp. This latter it acquired through its control over Barclays Bank which it had secured a few months earlier. With disinvestment having brought Anglo more than 65% of First National's equity and 76% of Samcor's, who can blame them for laughing all the way to the bank!" asked Duncan Innes in a *Leadership* article in 1988.

If there was serious doubt about short-term effectiveness, the possibility existed that the long term might be a different matter. In *Sanctions Against Apartheid,* published in 1989 (CASE, edited by Mark Orkin) Innes quotes a local businessman who put his finger on the weak link in SA's position: "The SA economy needs links with the rest of the world. There is a limit to the amount of capital the country can generate internally to finance growth. Also, the economy needs the technological links with the rest of the industrialised world. Without these links, the economy will very soon lose much of its competitiveness."

By 1990, President FW de Klerk was winning the diplomatic battle against Mr Mandela as both travelled the world and sanctions came under international review. The ANC maintained its rhetorical position but this was one battle it lost in a field where it had previously outperformed its opponent. The field was diplomacy. As a Cosatu unionist told Riaan de Villiers in a 1988 *Leadership* interview:

"Sanctions is a very important part of the platform of the whole international anti-apartheid community – perhaps its most important part. And to take up a vacillating or more subtle position on sanctions would be regarded as taking up a vacillating position on the liberation movement itself – which in many ways it would be."

SANCTUARY

Nonviolent activists often need a place of safety, normally from harassment, arrest or violence, where the opponent cannot reach them without violating religious, moral, social or legal prohibitions. In the US an extensive programme, based in churches and synagogues co-operating with secular counterparts, provides sanctuary to Central American refugees whom the US government treats as illegal immigrants.

In SA churches have publicly given sanctuary to squatters whose dwellings have been demolished; also, less publicly, to other victims of injustice, for instance community leaders fearing detention.

In 1980 a group of Crossroads women sought sanctuary in St George's Cathedral in Cape Town, to protest against continuous harassment and "repatriation" by the authorities.

In September 1988, the UDF's Murphy Morobe and Mohammed Valli Moosa and the NECC's Vusi Khanyile escaped from police custody and sought refuge in the United States Consulate in central Johannesburg. Detained since July 1987 – Khanyile since December 1986 – the three escaped from the Johannesburg hospital where they had been taken for treatment under police guard. (See *X factor*)

■ *THE Sowetan* has reported on the chasm between the white inhabitants and the black people of the Messina area after the conclusion of the marathon security trial in the town.

When the trial began, a Dutch Reformed Church minister, the Rev Lesiba Matsaung, in the township of Nancefield offered the families of the two accused sanctuary in the church house. Women's groups of various denominations came together and offered to cook food and look after the two families.

But at the same time Mr Matsaung was accused by the white sister church in the town of being supportive of "terrorists" and he is to appear before the church circuit to answer the allegation.

He is, however, unperturbed. "I am on God's mission to minister to the needy," *Sowetan* reported.

– Cape Times, 12.5.88

■ SIT-IN ENDS AS TWO ARE ARRESTED

THE three sit-in fugitives walked out of the British Consulate in Durban yesterday afternoon and two of them were arrested as they stepped out of the lift.

They are expected to appear in court today on charges of high treason, a police spokesman in Pretoria said yesterday.

The third man, former Robben Island prisoner Mr Billy Nair, was carried out of the building shoulder-high by jubilant supporters to thunderous applause from a crowd of more than 1 000 in Field and Smith streets.

He became the only member of the original six who had sought sanctuary in the consulate in September to remain free last night.

UDF president Mr Archie Gumede and NIC executive member Mr Paul David were arrested and taken away through a back door by plainclothes policemen.

In October three others had left the consulate and had been detained. They are Mr Mewa Ramgobin, Mr George Sewpersadh and Mr M J Naidoo, who have already appeared in court facing treason charges.

Mr Nair said they had decided to leave the sanctuary of the consulate because of the withdrawal of their Section 28 detention orders by the Minister of Law and Order.

"We realised the possibility of us facing treason charges. We are prepared to face it as part of the struggle for a free South Africa," he said.

– Natal Mercury, 13.12.84

SATYAGRAHA

This is the term Gandhi used for what the West calls nonviolence or nonviolent direct action or passive resistance. The negative terminology is regrettable, as Adam Curle points out: we do not say to the people we love "I non-hate you".

Gandhi's satyagraha was distinguished from simpler forms of passive resistance by the nuances of thought and conviction that lay behind each decision. Francis Hutchins noted in *India's Revolution and the Quit India Movement*: "When Gandhi gave advice it was never a simple matter. He ordinarily supplied a hierarchy of recommendations, starting with what he considered ideally preferable, and ending up with what he considered better than nothing . . . . Gandhi did not confuse his recommendations: he ranked them carefully from top to bottom, offering advice to those who were receptive whatever their level of dedication and sophistication."

Gandhi was opposed to all violence and coercion but he considered violence preferable to cowardly inactivity. "I do believe that, where there is only a choice between cowardice and violence, I would advise violence . . . . I would rather have India resort to arms in order to defend her honour than that she should, in a cowardly manner, become or remain a helpless witness to her dishonour," he said.

Gandhi also accepted that the ideal of nonviolence "is never fully realised in life". But he condoned the use of a degree of force in boycotts, for example, when it was motivated by a desire to minimise coercion rather than by purely strategic considerations. "For my ambition is no less than to convert the British people through nonviolence, and thus make them see the wrong they have done India," he said.

Satyagraha, meaning "holding firm to truth", is a complex concept, operating on three levels: the secular, the religious and the mystical.

On the secular level, involving tactics like civil disobedience and strikes, Gandhi argued against coercion on the grounds that "it means we want our opponents to do by force that which we desire but they do not. And if such a use of force is justifiable, surely they are entitled to do likewise to us?"

Gandhi believed that political liberty was the freedom to obey one's own will and conscience, rather than the will and conscience of any other. That freedom was reached "only by suffering in our own persons until our opponents see the error of their ways and cease to harass us by trying to impose their will on us".

On the religious level, the goal of satyagraha is to love one's opponent even as one loves oneself – almost identical to the Christian injunction to love your enemies. Self-realisation for Gandhi involved the perception that one's own self is the "same soul" that partakes of God throughout creation.

Satyagraha becomes "soul force" when, on the level of mystical awareness, religious discipline opens one up to grace and makes one's position "true". Gandhi cited the case of the prophet Daniel, who effected a change in the behaviour of lions without doing anything, as an example of how "soul force" can bring "instantaneous relief". He believed, like Christ, that anything was possible to the satyagrahi, since there was "no limit to the power" of soul force.

"The underlying belief in this philosophy is that even a modern Nero is not devoid of a heart," Gandhi said. "The spectacle – never seen before by him or his soldiers – of endless rows of men and women simply dying without violent protest, must ultimately affect him. If it does not affect Nero himself, it will affect his soldiery. Men can slaughter one another for years in the heat of battle, for then it seems to be a case of kill or be killed. But if there is no danger of being killed yourself by those you slay, you cannot go on killing defenceless and unprotesting people endlessly. You must put down your gun in self-disgust."

Gandhi also said: "A satyagrahi bids goodbye to fear. He is therefore never afraid of trusting the opponent. Even if the opponent plays him false twenty times, the satyagrahi is ready to trust him the twenty-first time, for an implicit trust in human nature is the very essence of his creed."

He added: "As a satyagrahi I must always allow my cards to be examined and re-examined at all times and make reparation if an error is discovered." And: "The conditions necessary for the success of satyagraha are: (1) The satyagrahi should not have any hatred in his heart against the opponent; (2) The issues must be true and substantial; (3) The satyagrahi must be prepared to suffer till the end for his cause."

(Apart from the work of Gandhi himself, a useful reference on this subject is Narayan Desai's *A Hand-Book for a Satyagrahi – A Manual for Volunteers of Total Revolution* published by the National People's Committee of Rajghat, Varanasi)

SILENCE

Individuals or groups may use silence as a method of expressing moral condemnation. This is most effective on formal occasions.

■ PUPILS REFUSE TO SING FOR MINISTER

SOME teachers at an Oudtshoorn primary school fear that the authorities may act against them after pupils refused to sing and dance for the Minister of Education and Training, Dr Gerrit Viljoen, at the school's opening ceremony.

One of the teachers involved, Mr Zolile Jingqi, who has been detained on several occasions, has been asked by the authorities to give written notice as to why the students did not participate in the activities of the day.

Mr Jingqi told *Grassroots:* "I called the choir and told them that we must rehearse because the school is to be officially opened. They said they will not sing.

"The pupils were even called to the staff-room where they stated very clearly that they will not sing for a person who was part of banning their organisations and declaring the state of emergency."

– Rural Focus, A Grassroots special report, October 1987

SIT-IN

A sit-in is a form of occupation used by workers on strike and other activists.

■ SIT-IN STUDENTS WIN VOICE ON SENATE

A two-and-a-half-hour occupation of the administration block at Rhodes University, Grahamstown, yesterday won for black students the right to present their views directly to the university senate.

This will make the Black Student Movement (BSM) at Rhodes the first such organisation to receive representation at that level of university authority.

Yesterday 300 students occupied the administration block for two-and-a-half hours . . . .

After consultation on both sides, the university agreed to accept the 10-person BSM executive at the senate.

– Weekly Mail, 3.4.87

SLOGANS

Short, catchy phrases that express a hope, aim or point of principle are part of most resistance struggles. "No taxation without representation" was the slogan of the American rebels who fought the British for independence, a slogan used in SA by Cosatu.

"The culture of South African democracy has become more than anything a culture of slogans – the short, sharp galvanising phrase has triumphed in the struggle over the patiently formulated thesis," *Weekly Mail's* Ivor Powell reported in 1989.

In a report on the Soccer City rally to welcome home the recently released "Sisulu Seven", Powell described Raymond Mhlaba as a man with "no sense of the showbiz of politics in the 1980s, less of how much the struggle for which he sacrificed nearly 30 years of his life had changed".

Contrasting the academic approach of the "Sisulu Seven" with toyi-toying audiences no longer willing to be politely attentive, Powell suggested that the phenomenon may be explained in part by the "nature of SA's ANC-supporting constituency". For some years – in recognition of the high rate of illiteracy in the working class – it has been strategy especially in the trade unions to educate through posters and slogans. In this way it was hoped that unity and organisation would be promoted within the working class. Along with "An injury to one is an injury to all" and "One country, one federation", "Organise, Mobilise" was one of the earliest and most influential of Cosatu's slogan campaigns.

"How successful this kind of approach has been was clearly to be read on practically everybody's back and chest at Sunday's rally." (*Weekly Mail*, 3.11.89)

SQUATTING

Within a few years of building their fort at the Cape in 1652, the Dutch were complaining about the Khoikhoi living and grazing their flocks on "company land". Ever since then, and more particularly since the Native Land Act of 1913 (which dispossessed black people on a massive scale), the Natives (Urban Areas) Act of 1923 (which severely restricted black access to towns and cities), and the Group Areas Act of 1950, black South Africans have been wished away and sometimes whisked away to the homelands, only to return to the cities and the struggle for shelter.

One of the results has been mass urban squatting in "informal settlements", garages and township backyards – an act of sheer necessity, but also a sustained, extensive and courageous form of civil disobedience in the face of armed raids, repeated demolitions, imprisonment and "deportation".

The Urban Foundation estimated that some seven million people were squatting in urban areas by August 1988.

STAYAWAY

This method of non-cooperation can have enormous impact when practised on a mass scale, not least because it acts like a barometer of political opinion in a country like SA, where the majority of people are disenfranchised.

In times of intense conflict, a stayaway may become a "stay-at-home", with people staying indoors to reduce the chances of "incidents" while demonstrating to the opponent the degree of unity and discipline among the protesters.

This method has been used in SA on several occasions. For instance, there was a one-day stayaway on June 26 1950, to protest against the Group Areas Act and the Suppression of Communism Act (then the Unlawful Organisations Bill), and also to mourn those who had lost their lives in the struggle – including 19 killed by police on the preceding May Day in Benoni, Orlando, Alexandra and Sophiatown.

According to an organisers' report on this stayaway: "While we did not achieve the desired results on this historic day, we, however, feel quite satisfied that the people of South Africa are behind us.

"This was demonstrated by a complete stoppage of work in PE, Uitenhage, Durban, Ladysmith, Evaton and Alexandra Township. Partial stoppage of work took place at the following centres: Johannesburg and the Witwatersrand, Danhauser, Bloemfontein, Grahamstown, Cape Town and other centres . . . . The people of Durban suffered most in that about 1 000 workers were dismissed from employment." (*From Protest to Challenge*, edited by Karis and Carter, Hoover Press, 1973)

After the shooting of 69 unarmed protesters at Sharpeville, and "about five" others in Langa, Cape Town, on March 21 1960, a stayaway began in Cape Town which was to last for the next three weeks.

"It was almost total, bringing many businesses and industries to a standstill . . . . Meanwhile, a day of mourning had been called for March 28 by both the ANC and PAC. Following this day the stay-at-home spread to other cities. It remained strongest in Cape Town, where it was 95% successful. In PE and Johannesburg it was 85 to 90% successful and in Durban 20 to 25%, with Indian support." (*The Theory and Practice of Black Resistance to Apartheid* by Mokgethi Motlhabi, Skotaville, 1984)

■ 2M PEOPLE IN STAYAWAY: PROTEST BIGGEST IN SA HISTORY – COSATU

MORE than two million workers and pupils took part in a national stayaway yesterday as voters went to the polls.

According to Cosatu general secretary Mr Jay Naidoo, the stayaway was the largest in SA history, with participation most marked in the PWV region.

Associated Chamber of Commerce spokesman Mr Vincent Brett said: "The stayaway is obviously very, very substantial."

Mr Naidoo said: "The significant thing is that more people have taken action in opposition to apartheid than have voted in the elections."

Pretoria was hit by a "virtually 100%" black stayaway yesterday, the general manager of Pretoria's Chamber of Commerce, Mr Alec de Beer, said. Most of the big industry in Pretoria comes under Cosatu and most of the big plants are shut until tomorrow due to an agreement with employers.

Streets in Soweto and Johannesburg were yesterday quieter than on Tuesday as many big businesses came to a standstill. According to the Durban Metropolitan Chamber of Commerce, it appears that large companies were hardest hit with up to 95% of the black workforce staying away in some cases.

Cape Town employers were reluctant to supply information . . . .However, estimates from Cosatu say that more than 50% of workers stayed away in the Western Cape.

Industry virtually ground to a halt in East London, with a Frame Group spokesman saying a 100% stayaway had cost the company two full production days.

– *Cape Times, 7.9.89*

■ WHAT'S REMARKABLE IS THAT IT HAPPENED

THIS week saw the first three-day nationwide stayaway in SA in 27 years. Other stayaways have taken place since 1961 but have been limited to two days.

The significance of this week's action lies as much in the fact that it took place at all as it does in the number of workers who stayed away.

Conditions militated against such a stayaway: it occurred in a period of protracted repression, restrictions placed on unions and political organisations, and regulations preventing organisations calling for a stayaway. In addition, the State and employers threatened harsh action against participants.

The aim of the "days of protest" was to demonstrate the depth of opposition to the Labour Relations Amendment Bill, the state of emergency and restrictions on political, youth, community, union and other groups.

The stayaway resulted in a government minister expressing willingness to discuss the content of the law . . .

The Labour Monitoring Group surveyed the extent of the stayaway by telephoning management throughout the metropolitan areas. . . .

A representative of the Association of Chambers of Commerce indicated the stayaway would cost about R500-million.

General comment on the success of the stayaway is restricted in terms of emergency regulations. Despite the emergency, however, the unions can be well satisfied with this demonstration of power.

Cosatu estimates from transport statistics that 1.9 million people who would have used mass transport on Monday failed to do so.

This figure, supplemented by an estimated 1 million people who did not use taxis as normal, gives Cosatu a total of 3 million workers staying away.

– Weekly Mail, 10.6.88

■ ONE MILLION STAYED AWAY IN WHITES-ONLY VOTE PROTEST

MASS stayaways in townships countrywide and a sudden upsurge of political violence made yesterday's poll quite different from any white election held to date – and ensured even before the votes were counted that May 6 1987 would have a special place in the history books.

More than one million people stayed away from work and school yesterday in protest at the all-white election and the suppression of trade unions and political organisations under the state of emergency, according to the estimates of the independent Labour Monitoring Group.

The stayaway, which began on Tuesday with an estimated 520 000 participant workers, affected all major centres with the exception of Cape Town and Bloemfontein.

– The Star, 7.5.87

STRIKE

When workers withdraw their labour power they may be staging a symbolic, short-term demonstration of worker unity and strength, or an attempt to stop production for a lengthy period, to cause sufficient economic disruption and hardship to the employer to bring about accession to their demands. Strikes are sometimes accompanied by picketing (where workers try to prevent strike-breakers or "scabs" from entering their workplace), and may also involve sit-ins (where workers occupy the workplace but don't work).

Until 1979, black workers in South Africa did not enjoy the formal, legal right to unionise or go on strike. Despite this, strikes have historically represented an important means whereby black workers have expressed both economic demands (improved wages and working conditions) and political dissatisfaction (protest against government policies and social conditions).

Throughout the 1970s, the mushrooming of "illegal" black trade unions was accompanied by successive waves of unofficial strike action. The tenacity and militancy of such worker action led to the Wiehahn Commission's report and the passing of the new Labour Relations Act in 1979. Through this, black workers were for the first time granted the right to form recognised trade unions and the right to embark on a legal strike.

The new legislation sought to curb the frequency and militancy of strike action by requiring workers and their unions to go through lengthy and complicated bureaucratic procedures before embarking on legal strikes. Despite this, the 1980s saw almost daily strike action. Most concerned wages, but union recognition disputes also featured prominently, as did strikes in protest against disciplinary action taken against fellow workers.

Two of the most significant strikes of this period occurred in 1987, when over 20 000 railway workers (members of the SA Railways and Harbours Workers Union) struck for over two months, and a dramatic 340 000 mineworkers (members of the National Union of Mineworkers) engaged in an historic three-week battle with the Chamber of Mines.

One of the longest strikes in the 1980s was that of the Sarmcol workers in Natal. A study of this strike reveals some of the major features which characterise strikes in South Africa – for instance their link to community support action – and shows also how strikes can give birth to new forms of democratic organisation.

In April 1985, close to 1 000 workers at the Sarmcol rubber factory in Howick, Natal, went on strike. Soon after the strike began, management sacked the entire workforce. But as far as the workers and their union were concerned, they remained on strike. An industrial court judgment found in favour of the company in 1987, but legal appeals against this finding were still taking place in 1989.

The primary cause of the strike was the failure of the union (Metal and Allied Workers Union) and BTR Sarmcol to conclude a full recognition agreement, but grievances also centred around retrenchments and workers' perceptions of harsh working conditions and the arbitrary powers of management.

Given the importance of Sarmcol as a major employer among the community of the nearby township of Mpophomeni, it was natural that strikers would turn to their community for support. In the months following, strikers organised community meetings and gathered support for a boycott of white shops in the Howick area. Support groups were formed in Maritzburg and Durban to raise funds and to mobilise support to deal with the problem of strike-breakers. Joint marches of students, youth and workers were organised in nearby townships, while in June

Ten people who speak make more noise than ten thousand who are silent. – Napoleon Bonaparte

1985, 92% of the workforce of Maritzburg engaged in a stayaway as an expression of support for the Sarmcol workers.

The strikers were creative in their efforts to publicise their struggle and mobilise support on a national level. Stickers and pamphlets were distributed and a slide-tape show was prepared to help educate people on the Sarmcol workers' struggles. Workers held a press conference and staged pickets outside BTR Sarmcol's head office in Johannesburg.

The hardship of the Sarmcol strike was also a source of innovation for new forms of worker organisation. Towards the end of 1985, the Sarmcol Workers' Co-operative (SAWCO) was started. In the words of one shop steward, this was a means of "teaching our children about democracy". SAWCO comprised five co-ops: T-shirt production, bulk buying, agriculture, a health clinic and a cultural project. The cultural project produced a play, entitled *The Long March*, which was used to gain nation-wide moral and financial support for the strikers.

Strikes represent an essentially nonviolent means of pressing for worker demands, but in South Africa they are often bitter and brutal. In the case of the Sarmcol strike, there were instances of clashes between police and striking workers and their supporters, and attacks on and killings of strike-breakers. In December 1986, three leading Sarmcol activists were abducted and murdered, allegedly by Inkatha-led vigilantes.

(D Bonnin and A Sitas: "Lessons from the Sarmcol Strike", in W Cobbet and R Cohen (eds): *Popular Struggles in South Africa*, Africa World Press Inc, 1988)

■ STRIKE ACTION ON THE INCREASE

THERE was an overall increase in the frequency, size and ferocity of strike action this year and a total of 3 097 220 man-days were lost as a result of strikes, according to the annual Review on Labour Relations in SA conducted by Levy, Piron and Associates.

In addition, 57 830 man-days were lost because of lock-outs and three million man-days were lost because of political stayaways, most of which related to the campaign against the Labour Relations Amendment Act which culminated in a three-day national stayaway at the time of the September elections.

The report says that large clashes on a national scale, such as those between SA Breweries and the Food and Allied Workers Union, and SA Transport Services and the SA Railway and Harbour Workers Union, as well as minor disruptive forms of industrial action, continued this year.

Periods of rapid union growth and the climate of political change and uncertainty were two factors which influenced the incidence of strike action this year, the report says.

A total of 76,9% of strikes were triggered by wage demands, 5% over recognition and retrenchment, 3,5% over dismissal, 2,3% over grievances and discipline and 12,3% over other issues.

In conclusion, the report says that strikes were likely to continue to be a commonly identifiable feature of the SA economy. And organised labour would be one of the most important forces in any future negotiations regarding a new political order in the country.

– The Star, 28.12.89

SYMBOLIC ACTION

Objects or actions symbolising a grievance can be used to focus and advance the views of protesters. For instance, the Free the Children Alliance used keys to highlight its 1987 campaign to "open the doors of apartheid jails".

In Prague in November 1989, a crowd of 300 000 gathered in Wenceslas Square "rattled keys to signify the bell that will toll the end of the regime, producing a vast, shimmering metallic roar that undulated repeatedly across the giant square". (*Cape Times*, 21.11.89)

In Cradock, when night-soil removal services stopped after the collapse of the community council, young activists solved the problem by dumping the full buckets at Administration Board offices.

■ DUMMY USED IN PROTEST FOR TEACHERS

A GAGGED dummy was placed at the speaker's table in a Rondebosch church last night to symbolise teachers silenced in terms of legislation preventing them from criticising any government department.

The sight of the dummy greeted an audience who attended a meeting on education organised by Education for an Aware SA (Edasa) and the Cape Democrats.

– *Cape Times, 15.6.89*

■ 'SYMBOLIC' OBJECTS OFFERED AT MASS

PRETORIA. – Objects representing violence in SA were "offered" before communion at a Mass held in Mamelodi East near here yesterday during a meeting of the Southern African Catholic Bishops' Conference.

During the Mass, dedicated to peace, black and white congregants offered rubber bullets, teargas canisters, a quirt, sjamboks, two petrol-filled bottles, stones and a knobkierie.

The objects were then symbolically dumped in a rubbish bin.

– *Natal Mercury, 27.1.86*

■ FINE FOR PROTEST AT JAIL DEATH OF CHILD

TWO mothers who chained themselves to the gates of parliament in protest against the death in detention of 12-year-old Johannes Spogter of Steytlerville, were yesterday fined R50 (or 25 days) in the Magistrate's Court.

Mrs Beverley Runciman, 34, of Zeekoevlei, and Mrs Cornelia Bullen-Smith, 31, of Muizenberg, previously admitted chaining themselves to gate 4 of parliament with placards on their backs reading "A Child has Died in Detention" and "We are Horrified at his Death".

– *Cape Times, 17.10.85*

■ DONKEY DEMO BY SQUATTERS

IN A symbolic plea for a home, an evicted squatter yesterday led a donkey carrying his wife and two of his three children to the steps of the Cape Town City Hall, watched by thousands of Christmas Eve shoppers thronging Darling Street.

He said he did not want to cause a sensation by his demonstration, but thought that at this "time of goodwill" his and similar people's troubles could be remembered.

Mr Moegamat Dunn's troubles began three years ago when he was living with his parents in Factreton Estate.

He was told by the City Council's housing department that as a married man he could not live with his parents. . . .

"Ever since then I have been living in squatter camps or wherever there was some kind of a roof over our heads," he said.

– Cape Times, 25.12.75

■ SOARING BALLOONS

THOUSANDS of coloured balloons soared into the sky yesterday as the Free the Children Alliance was launched in Cape Town.

A message attached to each balloon urged South Africans to speak out against the "squandering and brutalisation of the lives of our children, the nation's most important asset".

The messages, printed on yellow cards, rained down on Peninsula gardens as the balloons, a gift from the Greens movement in Germany, deflated.

Mrs Mary Burton, spokesman for the Alliance and Black Sash national president, said Family Day was "an appropriate day to express concern for children in prison under security legislation or emergency regulations".

– The Argus, 21.4.87

RIGHT
Free the Children balloons in Cape Town in April 1987.

Courtesy of THE ARGUS

TAKING OVER

Activists sometimes create platforms by interrupting a meeting, church service or other gathering to challenge the views being expressed, introduce new ideas or voice demands.

In Maritzburg in 1971, students protesting against the banning of Jesuit Father Cosmas Desmond chained themselves to the altar of St Mary's Church and interrupted another service at St Alphege's to address the congregation on "the complacency of the church". *(The Argus,* 6.8.71)

During the 1985 state of emergency, activists on the Reef began to use the trains taking workers to and from their jobs as mobile venues for political meetings (see *Camouflage).*

In Durban in March 1986, over 100 parents and pupils took over a crisis control course for teachers attended by the assistant director of education and training in Natal, Mr D du Toit.

They prevented Mr Du Toit from leaving because they feared he would call the police, and drew his attention to issues they felt were more urgent than the crisis control course.

Mr Du Toit undertook to request the release of three pupils arrested that week and to reinstate eight Lamontville teachers transferred to other schools. (*Natal Mercury*, 22.3.86)

The effect – if not the intention – of shows of solidarity with political defendants during trials has often been that courtrooms have been hijacked.

Walter Sisulu and some of his ANC comrades attended the trial of the "Broederstroom Three" in Johannesburg soon after their release; Archbishop Desmond Tutu blessed the "Yengeni 13" from the public gallery of the Cape Town Supreme Court in November 1989.

Clenched fist salutes, cries of "Amandla" and the singing of Nkosi Sikelel' iAfrika – both from the dock and the public gallery – have almost become part of courtroom routine.

UCT PROF CHALLENGES MISSIONARY'S SPEECH

BAPTIST missionary and alleged Renamo supporter Mr Peter Hammond was confronted at a meeting last night by the director of the Centre for Intergroup Studies at UCT, Professor HW van der Merwe, who accused him of distorting the truth.

Prof Van der Merwe made his challenge after Mr Hammond gave a speech to the Gospel Defence League.

Mr Hammond, who is a director of a group called Frontline Fellowship, was briefly imprisoned in Mozambique in October. He said doctrinaire Marxists in Mozambique hated the Christian church.

At the end of Mr Hammond's talk, Prof Van der Merwe stood up and said: "I have never heard such a distorted presentation in my life."

Prof Van der Merwe said he had read some of Mr Hammond's articles on Mozambique before visiting the country in May and had discovered them to be "untrue".

– Cape Times, 16.11.89

PEOPLE'S COUNCILLORS GOVERN ON 42ND HILL

THE nondescript Free State township of 42nd Hill, near Harrismith, looks like many other black areas in South Africa, but its politics are unique.

With a 49% poll in last October's municipal election – the highest turnout in the country for the poll – 42nd Hill is probably the only township where councillors enjoy substantial support from their community.

The high turnout came about as a result of months of talks between local activists and the official structures, consultations which have continued after the election.

Local activist Makhosini Msibi, an executive member of a "progressive" civic body, the Development Committee, said there had been a growing dissatisfaction in the township against councillors as early as 1985.

The residents' grievances centred on overcrowding, shortage of houses, the installation of electricity and sewerage, high rents and service charges, incompleted projects and lack of facilities.

"We felt we should form a civic association comprising students, youth and workers to mobilise residents on these issues," said Msibi.

A community organisation called Vuka Afrika (Africa Awake) was formed in 1986 with members drawn from youth and student congresses, he said.

But when the state of emergency was declared in June 1986, activists were harassed and detained, and the students refused readmission to schools and colleges after their release.

As a result Vuka Afrika collapsed at a time when dissatisfaction towards councillors was increasing, with widespread reports that the former town council had borrowed money from the Orange Vaal Development Board for projects which were not carried out or completed.

When last year's municipal elections were announced, a number of activists held discussions to work out a strategy to oust the old council from office.

"The basic idea was to set up some of our people in the council to create a platform," Msibi said. "We needed the platform because every time we set up a civic structure, the system was out to crush us.

"Much as we reject community councils, it was felt that, as a strategy, the council should be used to address residents' problems."

Seven new candidates, who stood as individuals, were voted on to the council, out of eight contested wards.

Mayor of the new council Johannes Mosikili said the new council's first task was to check finances, loans and projects undertaken by the old council.

"We discovered that the old council has acquired a loan of R2,9m from the Development Board. R1,6m of this is unaccounted for," Mosikili said.

"We decided to resign as a council as we could not make any progress with the present financial set-up and went back to the community to inform them of our position."

At a mass meeting held early this year, the residents called on the council not to resign but to set up a consultation with the provincial administrator, local community structures and other outside bodies.

– Weekly Mail, 29.9.89

■ LEAVE THESE PEOPLE ALONE!

POLICE attempts to start a "non-political community council" in Hout Bay have been set back by progressive organisations in the small Cape harbour township.

Community workers in the area said a meeting called by police station commander R de Villiers last month fits in with the government's JMC strategy.

Pamphlets advertising the meeting said it would be "non-political".

The meeting was attended by about 100 people, many of them members of progressive organisations.

De Villiers, the only speaker at the meeting, said he could "get things right" in Hout Bay because he had "all the contacts". He had R30 000 to use immediately in the community if he was satisfied with the co-operation of residents.

A Hout Bay lawyer stood up to explain that the people of Hout Bay already had an organisation to represent them, and he was told to sit down "because De Villiers doesn't have much time".

Former Robben Island prisoner Eddie Daniels, who lives in Hout Bay, then stood up to challenge De Villiers.

"You cannot say this meeting is not political," he said. "The fact that it is held in a coloured group area makes it political.

"Our community worker, Dick Meter, was detained for the community work he does in Hout Bay. If you, Mr De Villiers, want to be the new community worker in Hout Bay, then you must also be arrested.

"We have full confidence in our committee. They are accountable to the community. To whom are the police accountable?" he asked.

– New Nation, 4.12.86

TALKS

In a divided society, particularly one hamstrung by laws outlawing persons, bodies and points of view, an exchange of ideas, perceptions and feelings across political and legal barriers represent a creative form of intervention.

For SA, the most significant of these exchanges have been the series of visits to Lusaka by academics, businessmen, trade unionists, homeland leaders and others to talk with representatives of the banned ANC. These initiatives began in 1984 and continued until late 1989.

In themselves a form of nonviolent action, these visits have also been characterised by attempts to persuade the ANC to abandon armed struggle.

In a letter to President PW Botha, reported in *The Argus* on 12.4.88, Archbishop Desmond Tutu said: "You know I went to Lusaka twice last year. I tried to persuade the ANC to suspend the armed struggle. That is a matter of public record."

Perhaps the most celebrated of these talks was the meeting between Afrikaners and an ANC group in Dakar, Senegal, organised by the Institute for a Democratic Alternative for SA (Idasa).

The "spirit of Dakar" has been interpreted as the element binding a number of other organisations and initiatives such as the Five Freedoms Forum, which took more than 100 people to Lusaka in June 1989 to discuss the role of whites in a changing society.

At the Paris Indaba of November 1989, considered the successor to Dakar, talks began to turn into talks-about-talks: discreet pre-negotiation positioning sessions without the element of protest, publicity and defiance that had characterised Dakar. So successful were the talks that even *Business Day* editor Ken Owen, an adherent of "total war in debate", came out in favour of a nonviolent method: conciliation.

■ EVERYONE'S DUTY NOW IS TO SEARCH FOR CONCILIATION

THERE was a moment outside Paris last week, during the conference at Marly-le-Roi, when it became clear to me that in SA, at this time of momentous world-wide dislocation, it is not enough to win the arguments.

A heavy duty rests on every one of us to search diligently through the debris of communist ideology for conciliation.

The realisation – less than epiphany, more than an intellectual insight – came as I listened to the flat SA accent of Albie Sachs, the broken-bodied victim of a car bomb whom I had regarded for nearly 30 years as a fanatic and a killer, a high priest of the doctrine of the violent seizure of power – what we would today call a Stalinist.

When he was freed from prison and immediately went to run on the beach (was it 1964? and was it Clifton?) I noted the fact without emotion. I cared nothing for the man, only the principle that nobody should be imprisoned without trial.

Even when he was maimed by the bomb in Maputo, I refused to trivialise a life dedicated to revolution by making a display of shock. Live by the sword, I said, so die by the sword.

The rules of the conference and the laws of SA forbid me to quote Sachs but I found myself, astonished, in agreement with him. The people of this country have accumulated enough suffering to deserve freedom; none of us needs tyranny to replace tyranny.

Somehow a way must be found, and soon, to make this country safe and free for all its people, and to bring our scattered children home.

Sachs took the risk of dropping his ideological guard in the presence of his own ideological constituency; I could do no less. That night I rewrote the draft of my own contribution to the conference, abandoning the habit of brute intransigence – total war in debate – which is my personal style, and casting my arguments in a form that, I thought, might invite constructive response.

– Ken Owen, *Cape Times*, 6.12.89

■ THERE'S NO TURNING BACK

PARIS. – A week of debate here has significantly altered the future of SA – it's as simple as that.

On two major points, the ANC on one hand and Cosatu on the other, changed attitudes as irreversibly as the collapse of the Berlin Wall.

Who made the best speeches? It is difficult to say, but most delegates would single out Cosatu economist Mr Alec Erwin for making the most dramatic, and ANC constitutional researcher Mr Albie Sachs for his brief comment on human rights, which made even the normally intransigent editor of *Business Day*, Mr Ken Owen, ameliorate his position.

UWC economist Professor Pieter le Roux put his finger on the main economic debate when he said it was how to get the mix of a mixed economy right. And the biggest gains of the conference were on the economics front, for a full day was spent in deep discussion of economic plans and philosophy.

This is when Mr Erwin made his dramatic input, declaring that old style command economy ideas had to change as they had shown they could not market their goods effectively.

Put in simple language, what he finally said means that Cosatu has abandoned a strict economic view and is more flexible, agreeing that some of the free market economic truths are more important than old political beliefs which essentially nationalised all business.

Yet he remained extremely critical of present government policy. He said the country had to get a coherent and useful science and technology programme, as it did not help if every university did its own thing; a decent manpower programme so that artisans were not trained in modules that removed some essential skills; find an environment policy that did not rape natural resources; change the education policy; get a tourist policy that was coherent and so on, all of which should be done democratically with worker input.

– *The Argus*, 2.12.89

SMALL COASTAL TOWN
SHOWS THE WAY TO PEACE

A TINY coastal village is forging ahead with its own brand of platteland detente – with remarkable success.

It took years of racial strife, several unrest deaths and a consumer boycott to pave the way to the negotiating table.

But now, with prejudices and mistrust relegated to the back row, black and white community leaders of Port Alfred are talking their way to peace and a new future.

A boycott in the town lasted less than a week before it was brought to an end around the bargaining table.

Concerned businessmen reacted sharply to the sanctions threat. Under the auspices of the local Chamber of Commerce, they formed a new body – the Port Alfred Employers' Federation – and called on black leaders to come down from the shabby township that was once tagged "the hill of shame" after a newspaper report exposed the squalor and poverty in which its estimated 8 000 residents live.

They came, and amid both groups a new spirit of awareness began to emerge. But the talks did not end after the boycott was called off. Now there are eager moves in the town to build a community in which all races can live in harmony.

Mr Charles de Bruin, president of the local Chamber of Commerce, said: "We have been inundated with requests from neighbouring municipalities to share our formula for success. In essence, what we have done is nothing more than common sense.

"We discovered early on in our initial talks that it was futile negotiating with blacks who were not regarded as leaders by members of their community.

"We sought out the true local leaders and invited them to talk. We were astounded by their willingness to co-operate. We firmly believe that through harnessing our joint resources we have made the first tentative steps towards reform, albeit on a local level."

Mr Gugile Nkwinti, chairman of the Nonzamo Students and Guardians Association, agrees that the talks have been fruitful.

Mr Nkwinti, a UDF member, was detained hours after the declaration of the state of emergency but was released one week later.

"Once we started talking openly and honestly we cleared the way to what will hopefully prove to be a better future.

"There is still a long way to go but at least a start has been made. The white community leaders reacted positively to some of our demands that were within their control.

"On others, they opened up channels through which we could discuss our grievances directly with other government organisations.

"We fully realise we can only be effective as far as our own local community is concerned, but we hope that from this meeting will spring some goodwill and understanding that will, perhaps, serve as an example for the whole country," he said.

– Sunday Times, 18.8.85

TEA PARTIES

Former state president PW Botha stunned the world by having Nelson Mandela to tea at Tuynhuis, flying in the face of his own Total Onslaught/Total Strategy approach, shortly before he was forced to resign in 1989. The tea party may be described as PW Botha's single contribution to the idea of non-violence! Not that the idea was new . . . South Africans had been throwing tea parties for at least a year before PW hit on the idea.

■ TEA PARTIES WHICH ENRAGED POLICE

IN the last year of his life, David Webster presided over at least three tea parties for ex-detainees which were cut short by the security police.

At one of these, in Alexandra township, a Captain Van Haystings told Webster that "you will not have any more tea parties", according to detainee activists who witnessed the incident.

Webster, a founding member of the banned Detainees' Parents Support Committee and a commissioner of the Human Rights Commission (HRC), was assassinated nine days after a tea party was broken up by the police.

"More than once David was told that he would be held responsible for anything that happened at the parties," Max Coleman of the HRC said at Webster's funeral at the weekend.

Webster's last tea party, at St George's Church in Johannesburg on April 22, was disrupted 15 minutes after it began by Captain Van Haystings and two dozen security policemen during the singing of the anthem Nkosi Sikelel' iAfrika.

When the singing started, Van Hastings announced through a bull-horn that the meeting was being suspended because it was a "threat to law and order" under the emergency regulations.

"To say that the singing of Nkosi Sikelel' iAfrika was the reason for the termination of the meeting would be totally incorrect," a police public relations officer later said. "We are sure that the officer who issued the instructions did so after assessing the situation existing at the time."

Van Haystings later said that the meeting had not been banned because of the singing. He refused to say what aspect of the meeting had contravened the emergency regulations.

The security forces took an even tougher line at a tea party presided over by Webster at the NG Kerk in Alexandra last August.

Shortly after the meeting began, armed soldiers surrounded the church and security policemen called the meeting to a halt. "Van Haystings closed the doors and refused to let anyone enter or leave," said Steven Goldblatt, a lawyer who was present.

All those at the meeting, with the exception of foreign diplomats, were photographed and had their names and addresses taken.

The meeting was dispersed, and witnesses say Van Haystings told Webster, "You will not have any more tea parties." According to another lawyer, Thabo

Molewa, he was told that if he organised another party in Alexandra, he would be detained. Contacted for comment this week at John Vorster Square, Van Haystings said he had no problem about discussing the tea party issue. However, a superior officer would not allow him to comment, and would not comment in his own right.

A tea party in Webster's honour is planned for Johannesburg on May 27.

– *Weekly Mail, 12.5.89*

See also: Camouflage

TOYI-TOYI

The toyi-toyi emerged into public view during the marches and demonstrations of the youth that mushroomed into the Soweto Uprising of 1976. Since the early 1980s, few anti-apartheid occasions have passed without the dancing of the toyi-toyi, accompanied by songs, chanting and the shouting of slogans.

■ TOYI-TOYI AROUND PAUL KRUGER STATUE

PRETORIA. – Church Square, a shrine to Afrikaner nationalism, was the scene of an anti-apartheid protest by 1 000 people yesterday.

The event, around the statue of Paul Kruger, went off without a hitch. At one stage, police led away two white men to cheers from the crowd.

The demonstration started shortly before 1pm with a crowd of about 600 chanting, ululating, placard-waving protesters rhythmically dancing the toyi-toyi around Paul Kruger's statue in the centre of the square.

ANNA ZIEMINSKI

LEFT
A youth toyi-toyis after a political meeting in Johannesburg in June 1989.

139

Scores of policemen and hundreds of members of the public, as well as a large contingent of local and international journalists and diplomats, looked on.

Led by clerics, the procession soon swelled to about 1 000. There were no incidents in the biggest demonstration in Pretoria in decades.

– Cape Times, 16.9.89

■ FINGER-SNAPPING JAILHOUSE JIVE

PRISON warders' jaws must have dropped at the sight of the new dance that burst out in SA prison cells. Detainees jerked like puppets, threw their arms around, snapped their fingers and moved their feet and legs in swift and very staccato movements.

In the restrictive environment of prison, amid intense political discussion and debate, one can hardly think of a better way to lighten the atmosphere, and the dance was performed by young detainees to entertain themselves.

Now the dance – isikhando – has hit the township streets.

It is as much a political phenomonon as a social one, for isikhando is the latest in a line of dances which serve as a way for youths in the community to express themselves politically . . . .

The dance has spread from street corners to bus terminals, schools and yards of homes. But it is not popular in the nightclubs.

Here, s'thwela prevails – a modified version of an earlier sort of "statement".

The original form of this dance swept through the townships in 1987, causing an uproar in a community where repression and censorship are abhorred. It drew cries of "Censor!" and "Ban!"

Why? Because people were jumping on tables and chairs in the shebeens and shedding all their clothes. Some were inspired to such heights that they could be seen dancing naked on the roofs of houses in places like Mamelodi and Atteridgeville.

Experts say the dance originated from an ancient traditional dance called iFamo.

Jazz fundi Paul Maseko – a stern critic of the dance – says it went against African culture and tradition, for it was unheard of for dancers to strip completely naked in public places. Another expert agreed. The dance was traditional. But "it was mainly performed by women for old men. They would have a feast or a party, then move to a secluded place in the veld where the dance would be performed. The dance was very rhythmic and sexual but no one performed it completely naked."

These days the dancers no longer strip as they dance, at least not in the clubs where it is popular.

When dancing s'thwela the entire body moves around in a co-ordinated fashion while the waistline moves as if encircled with a hula-hoop. The legs are the pivotal point from which the entire movement is generated.

But when it began, with people snapping their fingers, throwing their arms into the air and screaming "S'thwela! Ayoyo!", the SADF was in the townships and drinking in the shebeens – repression, it seemed, was everywhere . . . .

The most resilient – and most overtly political of these "political" dances has been the toyi-toyi. Some say the toyi-toyi originated in the Eastern Cape at the height of the national protest in 1984/85. It goes with freedom songs and the chanting of political slogans.

Over the years as political songs and dances spread throughout the country, the toyi-toyi became more sophisticated and developed a number of variations of step and body movements.

Toyi-toyi is always danced in unison and the movements are determined by both the words and the rhythm.

"Heita, Mandela, heita" is sung as people lunge forward on one foot and then salute. A clap-in between the song is also included.

Poems can be recited during toyi-toyi and the rest of the crowd hums. "Woe betide Pietermaritzburg/Dark clouds gather over you," goes one sad song.

Dancers can lift their knees high in a military way or jive like some worshippers, depending on the song. In fact many of the less militant rhythms are adopted from hymns.

When "Wathint' abafazi wayi thint' imbokotho" is sung, the dancer's fingers point to the sky. A warning is sent out: "You have touched the women; you have dislodged a boulder; you will die."

Isikhando and s'thwela are popular now – but only with the youth.

But everyone – from tiny children to old ladies – can dance the toyi-toyi. This is not only because the steps are easy to do but also because the toyi-toyi, invented by youths, went beyond youth street culture. It was born of a movement that influenced the entire community – and is part of the community's cultural and political expression.

It is here to stay.

– Weekly Mail, 15.6.89

TRIALS

Attending trials as an observer may be a way of showing solidarity with the accused. Under reactionary regimes, recording and analysing proceedings and trends in the courts may be of value to popular struggles. Court monitors also play a role in helping accused people obtain legal representation or secure other rights.

The Black Sash monitored pass courts for decades. With the replacement of influx control measures like the dompas with "orderly urbanisation" regulations in 1986, their attention shifted to the increasing number of political trials (public violence, treason, etc), often involving juvenile accused.

Under conditions of restriction, statements made at political trials have provided some of the most telling commentaries on the SA struggle. "Ten years! My husband, it is nothing!" a woman called out from the public gallery at the moment of sentencing in a cry of solidarity that echoed around the country, while the question addressed to the judge by an ANC sympathiser jailed in 1987 likewise made a powerful political point: "I wonder what you would do, my lord, if you were in my position in our country?"

Apart from raising the awareness of the observers themselves, court monitoring can provide material useful to historians, educators and campaigning activists. It has been important in identifying widespread disenchantment with the current legal system and may play a role in reshaping it.

UNDERGROUND

When a government suspends the rule of law and imposes restrictions so that its opponents face detention and the banning of their meetings and communications, people are forced into either submission or secrecy.

The creation of alternative systems of communication has been used to counter the regime's control over information and ideas. In the Soviet Union, samizdat (self-publishing) first appeared in 1958, developing into a network, especially after the late 1960s.

Before perestroika and glasnost opened up legal space, over 30 samizdat periodicals were in circulation, with content varying from newsletters to trial transcripts, petitions, open letters, political analysis and literary work.

Carried on largely by dissidents belonging to human rights, religious or nationalist groups, samizdat survived despite a government ban on acquiring duplicating facilities, using printing equipment or operating printing presses.

In SA, activists often went underground during the state of emergency imposed nationally in 1986. They also had to hide resources like literature, and resort to secrecy in organising meetings.

■ UDF EMERGES TO CALL FOR JUNE PROTESTS

THE major target of the year-old state of emergency, the UDF, emerged briefly from the shadows this week to announce two weeks of protest action from June 16.

UDF acting publicity secretary Murphy Morobe appeared from hiding to hold a press conference in which he announced that the UDF had called for various forms of protest between June 12 and June 26.

Details of the protests may not be published in terms of the emergency regulations.

Morobe was speaking shortly after 200 delegates from the UDF's nine regions met in secret in Durban at the weekend for a national working committee conference to decide on the organisation's policies for the next two years.

– Weekly Mail, 5.6.87

HUSH-HUSH BIRTH OF A YOUNG GIANT

SOUTH Africa's most powerful single political grouping was launched this week-end – in such total secrecy that even the 100 delegates and the keynote speaker did not know until a few minutes before the launch exactly where it was going to happen.

With half-a-million signed-up members, Sayco is the largest single political organisation in SA history – one in every 60 of SA's 30 million people.

Launched just four days before the 45th anniversary of its predecessor, the ANC Youth League, Sayco is significant not only for its size, but because the launch – at Cape Town's UWC campus on Saturday – could take place at all.

In the last six months Sayco has organised and launched seven regional groupings in conditions of such secrecy that even sympathisers outside the youth movement were unaware until days afterwards that regional congresses had been launched.

For the national launch, a disinformation campaign – apparently carefully planned to confuse security forces – swung into action days before the gathering.

Some local delegates actually believed at different times last week that the launch had been postponed indefinitely, moved to Durban, lost its venue, had to shift venue locally three times in the space of almost as many hours.

And afterwards, at least one Cape Town activist insisted that the launch had not even taken place.

The result: delegates were safely back in home territory before news of the launch even began to leak through to the media.

"Before the first state of emergency, we were organising locally through open mass rallies," Sayco official Rapu Molefane said before the national launch.

"So when the crackdown came we were easy targets. Many of our officials and leading activists were picked up. But the organisation survived and by the second emergency we had learned our lesson.

"We are a legal organisation, operating legally, but we are working underground. When the June 12 crackdown came, it hardly touched our main structures."

– South, 2.4.87

HALT EVICTIONS CALL

HUNDREDS of pamphlets calling for a halt to evictions were distributed in Soweto yesterday.

At the time of going to press no political or civic association had claimed responsibility for the pamphlet whose significant portion cannot be quoted because of the emergency regulations.

– Sowetan, 22.4.87

See also: Camouflage, Sanctuary

UNMASKING

In SA, where several people identified as informers have been attacked and killed, a nonviolent way of dealing with security police and informers is to publish their names and photographs as soon as they are discovered and so neutralise them by making it difficult or impossible for them to continue secret activities.

■ CONFESSIONS OF A CAMERAMAN WHO GAVE PHOTOS TO THE POLICE

GREGORY Flatt's was a familiar face in journalist and activist circles in Cape Town. He took photographs on a freelance basis for the Cape Town weekly *South,* and was always at political meetings and press conferences.

This week he attended another press conference – with himself as the focus. Flatt, 21, was confessing to having been a paid police informer for the past two-and-a-half years.

The killings on election night last Wednesday, the "police attempt to cover up" and Lieutenant Gregory Rockman's outspoken criticism of police brutality had spurred him to take a decision he had long thought about, he said.

His face, wrapped in dark glasses, showed little emotion as he recounted how one of his specific tasks was to "get close to journalists" and find out their methods of operation and their sources.

"I also had to check on organisations' computer systems so that they (security police) could interfere." Another "task" was to steal computer disks to copy and replace afterwards. He claimed he had never in fact done this.

Flatt presented the pictures he took at rallies and meetings and of prominent activists to his security police handlers. "I also spent time identifying people in my own pictures as well as in other pictures they supplied," he said.

How did he become police informer number CW 935, code-named "Mark"?

He was in Std 9 during boycott-ridden 1985 and left school without writing his final exams. Active in Elsie's River youth organisations, he was twice arrested for being part of illegal gatherings, he said.

During 1986 he flew to Johannesburg, caught a train to Mafikeng and was arrested crossing into Botswana. He denied any intention of undergoing military training under the ANC but would have joined the ANC "if they had asked me".

After being handed over to SA security police he was transferred to Cape Town. During his detention he was "assaulted and threatened".

"They threatened to hold me under Section 29 indefinitely or charge me with illegal gatherings or public violence or leaving the country illegally.

"In return for spying I was offered release from detention as well as money."

On January 29 1987 he accepted the offer and was immediately released.

He earned about R500 a month.

This week MDM spokesperson Cheryl Carolus said there would be no retribution against Flatt.

– Weekly Mail, 15.9.89

POLICE SPY AT UCT UNMASKED

A UCT student and active member of Nusas yesterday confessed to being a police spy.

At a press conference at UCT, Mr Daniel Pretorius, a 19-year-old social sciences student, said his brief was to infiltrate Nusas and to supply information on it and the activities of Sansco and "any divisions between the two that could be exploited".

A police spokesman in Pretoria yesterday refused to comment, but UCT's vice-chancellor and principal, Dr Stuart Saunders, said he was seeking a meeting with the Minister of Law and Order, Mr Adriaan Vlok, on the matter.

Mr Pretorius said the state saw the potential power of the Nusas-Sansco alliance, which was truly non-racial, as "a huge threat" and that the security police "wanted to intensify these divisions".

Asked by the *Cape Times* whether he could name his security police contacts, Mr Pretorius said he could not do so without consulting lawyers.

He claimed he had accepted the security police offer out of "political naivety".

Mr Pretorius confessed his spying activities to Nusas and Sansco yesterday. They subsequently called the press conference.

– Cape Times, 12.8.87

RIGHT
Gregory Flatt confesses he was a police spy at a press conference in Cape Town in September 1989.

Courtesy of THE ARGUS

VIGIL

With prayer meetings, funeral services and fasts, vigils have come to be held as an expression of protest as well as solidarity with the victims of apartheid. The spirit of these vigils is captured in the Biblical injunction: "Pray for those in prison as though you were in prison with them." (Hebrews 13)

■ OVERNIGHT VIGIL FOR THE CHILDREN

WHILE the State President opened the new session of parliament on Friday, across the avenue some 30 other organisations presented an entirely different picture of SA.

Inside St George's Cathedral, organisations as diverse as the Call of Islam and the government-funded Child Welfare, maintained their overnight vigil calling for the release of all detained children.

During the 20 hours of prayers and discussions, national president of the Black Sash Mrs Mary Burton said it was "now possible in SA for a child of seven to be arrested, detained, charged, convicted and sentenced without the parents ever knowing".

– Sunday Times, 1.2.87

■ SASH HOLD VIGIL

BLACK Sash members kept a vigil at a Chesterville, Durban, home last night with mothers who say they have to protect schoolchildren from township vigilantes.

Mrs Ann Colvin of the Black Sash in Durban said yesterday members planned to keep watch over the children and their mothers who say they have been spending sleepless nights guarding their children against the "A Team".

"The violence by the 'A Team' has forced mothers in Chesterville to gather their children into a single house so that they can sleep," said Mrs Colvin.

. . . On Wednesday several mothers, some crying hysterically, telephoned a local newspaper for help, saying children were being forcibly abducted and taken to Street 13 in Chesterville where they alleged the "A Team" had their headquarters.

– Natal Witness, 30.5.86

ROGER MEINTJIES

RIGHT
A vigil for slain ANC cadre Ashley Kriel in Bonteheuwel, Cape Town, in June 1987.

VOLUNTARY EXILE

Protest may be expressed by abandoning an unjust or oppressive state, and living elsewhere, temporarily or permanently. This method is also called protest emigration, and, in India, hijrat, derived from the Arabic hejira which describes Mohammed's flight to Medina to escape the tyranny in Mecca. Gandhi believed there was nothing immoral about emigration if a satyagrahi could not bear repression, either morally or physically.

The democratic demonstrations in East Germany that toppled the government were preceded by mass emigration: the state started haemorrhaging when its citizens used tourist visas to neighbouring countries to escape to the West.

South Africa has sent thousands of its children into exile, ranging from those who run liberation movements from abroad, to activists escaping arrest, to the generation of black schoolchildren who left after the Soweto Uprising in 1976, to whites who could not stomach the system, to writers and artists who could not function under repression.

Repatriation became one of the ANC's conditions for negotiations in 1990.

147

WADING IN

Fighting them on the beaches has always been a particularly appropriate form of anti-segregation protest in SA "All of God's beaches for all of God's people" was the message conveyed by the MDM in the winter picnics of its 1989 defiance campaign – and by earlier protesters, who waded in literally as well as figuratively.

One was Labour Party leader the Rev Allan Hendrickse, who followed the lead of his son and fellow MP Peter on January 4 1987, by swimming at Port Elizabeth's "white" Kings Beach.

Mr Hendrickse paused at the edge of the surf to tell journalists: "We are definitely pulling out of the tricameral parliament if the Group Areas Act is not changed."

The attorney-general declined to prosecute Mr Hendrickse but President PW Botha gave him a public dressing-down and demanded that he apologise or resign from the cabinet. Mr Hendrickse apologised.

■ BLOUBERG BEACH MEMOIRS

THE MDM's Defiance Campaign had originally targeted the whites-only beach at the Strand. A full-scale military operation (shades of Churchill's "we will fight them on the beaches") rendered access to the area almost impossible.

The MDM nimbly diverted picnickers, setting the scene for the beach which gives the world its postcard image of beautiful Cape Town to reveal some of the city's ugliness too.

I grew up down the road from Blouberg, and most of my memories of it are unpleasant. Yet on August 19, Blouberg offered me a brief glimpse of the freedom we are all fighting for. Hundreds of people, black and white, simply having a good time on a sunny winter's afternoon.

Frisbees floated lazily through the air. Anti-military sandcastles were built. The beach was a carnival of games – everything from relatively serious football to hop-scotch. Mothers on large woollen blankets dispensed goodies to their laaities – this was, after all, ultimately a picnic.

A solitary banner proclaiming defiance looked almost incongruous amidst the tranquility. The arrivals from each new bus announced themselves with a friendly toyi-toyi, but the mood was more mellow than militant. Visions of the future tend to be short-lived in the present. After about half an hour, a police van drew up. Its occupants stumbled out, cocking their weapons and squinting their eyes at "the enemy".

No one took much notice, and the men in uniform began to feel a bit silly. They even let their weapons rest at their sides. The arrival of reinforcements, however, brought a new sense of purpose and they came charging at us across the sand, quirts flying.

Brandy-and-coke white trash gathered round their bakkies in the parking lot sought to lend a hand to those on duty.

One decided to show a Black Sash lady the spots on his bum. I doubt whether there is any group of South Africans more aware of their rights than the Black Sash. She promptly laid a charge and kept six policemen out of the fray for a good while.

In the protected environment of the MDM one tends to forget the racial attitudes of ordinary whites. A man in a bakkie asks me what's happening.

"The police have just chased black people off the beach with sjamboks," I explained, thinking that nobody could fail to identify with the victims of such a tale.

I overestimated white South Africans.

"But this is a European beach," he ventured.

"We're 10 000 kilometres away from Europe," I replied. "This is a South African beach and it belongs to all South Africans."

"It's been very nice talking to you," he concluded, as his foot eased off the clutch. Nothing if not polite.

– Tony Karon, *Upfront, November 1989*

■ PEACEFUL PROTESTS ON DURBAN BEACHES

DURBAN. – Five thousand anti-apartheid protesters of all races paddled into the Indian Ocean on a whites-only beach here on Sunday, while police kept a watchful eye from the sidelines.

The protest at Addington Beach, about two kilometres from the centre of Durban, was the latest move in a national defiance campaign.

The cheerful protest was in stark contrast to Saturday's scenes in Cape Town, where riot police used teargas and water-cannon filled with purple dye to disperse demonstrators from the city centre.

The Durban demonstrators, many of them wearing yellow caps with anti-apartheid slogans, arrived in a constant stream from mid-morning and were allowed past a chain of about 800 police officers, trucks and water-cannon ranged along the beach road.

"There are no incidents to report. We had ample numbers of police at the beach, but nothing happened," a police spokesman said.

However, police had to intervene between right-wing whites and protesters of all races on several occasions. About 12 middle-aged white men were seen carrying decorated sjamboks – "for later use", as one told a reporter.

One man was seen using his sjambok to threaten a small black child who was dipping his toes into the whites-only South Beach paddling pool.

– *Cape Times, 4.9.89*

■ SALDANHA BEACH PROTEST PEACEFUL

MORE than 2 000 people yesterday protested peacefully and without incident against beach apartheid at Saldanha Bay as part of the MDM's defiance campaign.

A Western Cape police spokesman said police were present but took no action against the marchers.

An MDM spokesman last night said the protesters had first held a service in the Anglican church next to the beach.

About 3.30pm the procession, led by clerics, moved off and marched past the whites-only sign on to the beach.

"About five right-wingers stood in our path, but as we approached them three moved off and the procession simply parted and marched past the remaining two," the spokesman added.

The protesters marched on a further 800 metres, then erected a sign in the sand stating "Away with Apartheid".

– Cape Times, 11.9.89

■ 1 000 IN PEACEFUL 3-HR BEACH PROTEST

A PROTEST lasting close to three hours went off at the Strand without incident today as more than 1 000 people walked along the length of the "whites only" beach to protest against beach apartheid.

The action culminated in a "service of thanksgiving" near the pier at the main parking lot where Archbishop Desmond Tutu and Dr Allan Boesak hailed the protest as "the opening of Strand beach".

Earlier in the day policemen wearing black PT shorts or tracksuit pants, T-shirts and with towels draped around their necks, attempted to mingle with the crowd. Their identity became clear when they started arresting camera crews and photographers who were taken to Strand police station where they waited for 15 minutes before walking out.

The protest started at 10.30am when about 300 people marched down the beach towards Cape Town and were halted by two police vans.

They were warned to disperse within ten minutes in terms of the Internal Security Act. Police said force, including firearms, could be used to disperse the crowd. However, the crowd spread and the warning was not put into effect.

Dr Boesak spent time on the beach with a group of supporters and later Archbishop Tutu, wearing white tracksuit pants, a blue T-shirt bearing the words "Call me Arch" and a sailor's cap, also arrived.

One or two braved the water and a man blew bubbles over the heads of the crowd. A border collie played with a frisbee while a group of protesters played a quick game of cricket and another unpacked a picnic basket for the family.

Although only two police vehicles went on to the beach, there were many vans and two armoured vehicles standing by. Many police vehicles and men with radios were hidden in side streets and some waited at a graveyard.

At a brief press conference Archbishop Tutu said: "If that was low-profile police presence then I'm Bing Crosby."

– Weekend Argus, 30.9.89

1 000 HOLD PROTEST PICNIC ON PE BEACH

PORT ELIZABETH. – About 1 000 people held an incident-free non-racial picnic on Pollok Beach here on Saturday, in protest at the fact that the beach has been reserved for whites only.

Loud cheers greeted the unveiling of a signboard declaring the beach open at 12.30pm by former city councillor and long-time proponent of open beaches Mr Graham Richards.

Police kept a low profile during the ceremony and there was a carnival atmosphere as the crowds danced, waved banners and sang freedom songs.

The ceremony started with a prayer by Bishop George Irvine of St John's Methodist Church. This was followed by a speech by the Rev David Vika of the Interdenominational African Ministers Association of SA.

– Cape Times, 2.10.89

They also surf who only stand and wade. – *Aging luminary of the bar at Muizenberg beach*

RIGHT
Protesters picnic at Durban's "whites only" Addington Beach in September 1989.

Courtesy of THE ARGUS

> **Taxation without representation is tyranny.**
> *– James Otis*

■ FW ORDERS OPEN BEACHES

PRESIDENT FW de Klerk yesterday declared all beaches in SA open immediately to all races. He asked that where this conflicted with local by-laws, the authorities should act "in the spirit of this decision".

Addressing the President's Council, Mr De Klerk also said the government planned to repeal the Separate Amenities Act "as soon as possible" but that certain "fitting measures" would be introduced in "a few sensitive areas" once this happened.

The government would soon enter discussions, both on a parliamentary level and with other interest groups, before deciding on such measures, he said.

One top government source suggested that inland water resorts, for example, might be exempted from the apartheid axe when the law goes. However, Mr De Klerk singled out beaches as a "specific area" where the government felt a decision could be taken immediately and implemented without delay.

Meanwhile, veteran apartheid-sign hacker Mr Morris Fynn has hung up his saw, claiming victory. "I was right all along and they were wrong," he said.

Mr Fynn, who has been arrested more times than he can remember for sawing down beach apartheid signs, will appear in court in January on another similar charge.

– Cape Times, 17.11.89

WITHHOLDING TAX

Citizens of various countries have deprived their governments of revenue by refusing to pay some or all types of taxes e.g. income tax, property tax, or by refusing to buy certain required licences. The refusal to pay tax or licence fees may be a protest against a particular injustice related to the particular tax or licence.

In the 1960s, singer/activist Joan Baez informed the US Internal Revenue Service that she did not intend to pay the 60% of her income tax that she calculated went to the defence establishment. The Archbishop of Croke advised the Irish to stop paying tax in 1887, saying: "I made the decision to begin withholding the military portion of my taxes only after much prayer, reflection and discussion with close friends."

A hundred years later Canon Paul Oestreicher, an office bearer of both the British Council of Churches and the Campaign for Nuclear Disarmament, faced charges for withholding the thirty tax pounds he calculated would go toward nuclear weapons.

In 1987 the SACC resolved to support Cosatu's stand on "no taxation without representation" and to investigate how to stop deducting pay-as-you-earn tax from council workers' salaries. It also advised church members that withholding tax was a "strong political act", carrying however equally strong penalties including sequestration and possible imprisonment. In 1990 the Conservative Party suggested that its members should stop paying for their TV licences in protest at SABC censorship.

WITNESS

In September 1985 a group of church workers and theologians living and working in the black townships around Johannesburg produced the *Kairos Document: Challenge to the Church* in response to what they called the kairos or "moment of truth" for the church in SA.

The document questioned the churches' failure to address the political crisis in SA, repudiated "state theology" that provided biblical justification for apartheid and called for a "prophetic theology".

The statement carried the signatures of some 150 theologians and church workers from a wide range of churches, and provoked widespread and continuing controversy. Revised and translated into a dozen languages, the Kairos Document became one of the best known and most vigorously debated theological statements in local ecumenical history.

An international version of the Kairos Document entitled *The Road to Damascus* (1989) has recently appeared, focusing on the implicit support for the national security state found among right-wing religious groups in countries such as the Philippines, Korea, El Salvador and SA.

"In 1988, the church in SA reached a turning-point in its witness against apartheid and the intensified violence against the majority of people in this country," SACC general secretary Frank Chikane told a mid-1988 Johannesburg conference where the drafting of a concrete programme of NVA was on the agenda.

■ THE CHURCH IN MEDITATION

TWO differing theological approaches within the SA Council of Churches could explain the group's difficulty in hammering out a programme of action against apartheid.

Addresses delivered by SACC general secretary Frank Chikane and president Manas Buthelezi at this week's conference in Johannesburg reflect the ecclesiastical and political dilemma facing the church.

In his keynote address, Chikane said the church was breaking new ground in confronting social realities.

He cited the march of church leaders in Cape Town on February 29 as an indication of this shift towards active protest. "There will be those who fear that we might be beginning to depart from the 'tested' tradition of the church, doing something that the church should not do.

"There will be those who are doubtful and who prefer not to try until they are sure about it (political involvement). This is natural and part of the struggle."

In a thoughtful speech, Buthelezi debated the theological implications of political action. He identified three ways of characterising the social role of the church:

● The "state church", where a great overlap exists between organised religion and government, and where clerics are manipulated by the state. The Ned Geref Kerk was in this position in SA, he said, and had been dubbed "the National Party at prayer".

● The "church state", in which political activism had established itself within church liturgy. Buthelezi referred to a "liturgical coup d'etat", represented most graphically by the politicisation of religious funerals. On some levels in SA, he

Am I willing to suffer with the people here, the suffering of the powerless, the feeling impotent? Can I say to my neighbours: I have no solutions to this situation; I don't know the answers, but I will walk with you, search with you, be with you.

– Ita Ford.

(Maryknoll sister assassinated in El Salvador in December 1980)

said, the "people in the pews" had "gone beyond" theologians concerned with matters of doctrine and practice.

● The "church under the cross", which adhered rigidly to the Gospel. In this view the church should and must take a stand publicly, even on controversial social questions, but only when it is empowered to do so by its special mandate."

At times in its history "the church was used as a pawn in political intrigues," said Buthelezi. "In gaining breathing space, the church lost its soul." He cautioned against the total politicisation of the church.

Chikane eschewed the intricacies of theological doctrine, choosing to stress the political crisis at hand. The latest declaration of the state of emergency, media restrictions, bannings and proposed labour and political legislation demanded a strong response from the church.

"In the face of the attacks from the state, various church groups and unknown forces of darkness, we (the SACC) are now called upon more than ever to reaffirm our commitment to the God of justice, peace and righteousness," he said. "Our obedience is to our God, and our God alone."

– Weekly Mail, 1.7.88

X FACTOR

Peter Storey, former president of the Methodist Church, once called the unforeseen, the unexpected, the surprise ending which no one can predict "the X factor".

Creative challenges and unexpected responses have proved to be powerful additions to the "arsenal" of NV activists. Surprise tactics on the part of police have been known to be equally disarming.

■ WOMEN COPS STOP MARCH

ABOUT 150 marchers led by Archbishop Desmond Tutu in a protest against the emergency regulations were surprised yesterday to be stopped in the city centre by a squad of policewomen.

Archbishop Tutu said later it was "a small feather in their cap" that the police had used women.

The multiracial squad was under the command of a woman lieutenant and seemed unarmed – a sharp departure from previous police action against banned demonstrations.

The march followed a service in St George's Cathedral held in solidarity with the MDM's defiance campaign.

When the service started, about 60 policewomen were standing in groups of about four at various points near the cathedral.

When the church leaders and other marchers emerged, the groups of policewomen moved in on the leading group.

Over the next 200 metres they were stopped about three times by policewomen who warned them that the march was illegal and that they should disperse.

The first warning was issued in a shaky voice by a coloured policewoman – which flabbergasted the marchers, who stopped.

At the intersection with Loop Street, the officer in control of the squad told the marchers to stop. Traffic slowed down and office workers looked on in amazement. At one stage the leading protesters knelt down on the pavement while the others sang.

When a news cameraman at one stage accidentally knocked off the hat of a policewoman she exclaimed: "Oh! My hat!"

Archbishop Tutu eventually agreed to lead the group back to the cathedral on condition no one was arrested. Back in the cathedral he described the march as "a victory for nonviolence".

– Cape Times, 18.8.89

■ SMASHING OPEN THE LOCKS WITH A WEAPON CALLED FARCE

FOUR men stroll out of detention in their pyjamas. They ensconce themselves in the German embassy. Another prisoner rises from his hospital bed – he flies to Johannesburg and the sanctuary of the US consulate. Six released detainees decide to protest against their restriction orders by reimprisoning themselves; they choose the British embassy. All of this occurs in SA within less than a fortnight.

The elements of high farce in the current spate of escapes from emergency detention are unmistakeable. Either SA detainees have suddenly acquired Houdini-like talents or the locks on their three-year-old traps have rusted. It is not so simple, of course: the explanation is of more far-reaching political importance.

Behind the bizarre sequence of events lies an innovative and concerted assault on a much hated practice that has grown too big and gone on too long.

Detention without trial is under attack from those most directly affected by it: the detainees themselves.

Just when it seemed emergency incarceration would go indefinitely – an estimated 33 000 people have been through detention cells since June 1986, some of them for close on three years – a combination of life-and-death hunger strikes and nonchalant escapes has threatened the system as never before.

It is a reflection, in the words of sources as diverse as the outlawed ANC and local liberal commentators, of the ability of the broad resistance movement to fashion new and surprising responses to ever-tightening conditions.

According to the government's own estimates, barely 300 people remain in detention and their cases are being reviewed as a matter of urgency. Although it is not about to disappear, the system has atrophied significantly.

Murphy Morobe is a pioneer of the high-profile "diplomatic route to freedom" tactic – he and UDF-aligned colleagues Mohammed Valli and Vusi Khanyile secured unconditional freedom after a five-week sojourn in the US consulate last year. His response to this week's events was that "people will always find creative ways to challenge the emergency; it is a fact the government has to live with".

The most dramatic example of this "creativity" – the nationwide hunger strike – has not only succeeded in pressurising Minister of Law and Order Adriaan Vlok into releasing hundreds of detainees; it has also refocused the attention of the world on SA's detention cells.

Emergency detention certainly did achieve the government's initial aim of taking vast numbers of key activists off the streets at a time of nationwide ferment; but now it seems the state may have to embark on a major tactical rethink.

One of the catalysts for the hunger strike was the fact that most long-term detainees did not even have the "stimulation" of interrogation – they were simply vegetating, and the pressure was becoming intolerable.

The hunger strike broke the stalemate. Detainees were moved to hospitals for urgent treatment, and as the conditions of their detention changed willy-nilly, opportunities for escape presented themselves.

Lawyers for Human Rights national director Brian Currin believes the hunger strike has been "a very successful strategy".

"It has succeeded in reminding the average citizen that there are people languishing in jail without trial. And the potential threat of some people dying in detention has resulted in the minister releasing people whom he would not normally have thought about, let alone released."

Currin cautions that the "brutalisation" of SA society is such that the public could become hardened to hunger strikes if the tactic is over-used.

The bids to secure the release of all detainees took a major step forward this week, with the decision by released but restricted detainees to stage a high-profile protest against their restriction orders.

This is also a tactic with a limited lifespan.

The six ex-detainees who have moved into the British embassy in Pretoria no doubt drew encouragement from the experience of the "German embassy four", whose diplomatic diversion brought more than mere release.

The release orders of Sayco members Ephraim Nkoe, Clive Radebe, Mpho Lekgoro and Job Sithole had been signed before their escape – and they included tough restrictions. But when they walked out of the embassy into the Pretoria sunshine, it was as completely free men.

Currin says this concession "illustrates the government's continuing sensitivity to international pressure".

It would be naive to conclude that the current attack on the detentions system will lead to its disappearance. It is sobering to note that while hundreds of detainees have come out since January, other activists have been taken in.

But the numbers game is important here: the emergency prison population has declined dramatically, and the hunger strike/diplomatic sit-in tactic is far from exhausted.

Dozens of prisoners are still refusing food, and the spectre of a hunger striker dying – thus becoming a martyr figure of the order of Steve Biko – is enough to convince the government of the need for compromise, despite catcalls from the Conservative Party.

For the moment the state is, in Morobe's words, "on the defensive" on the issue: the powerless in prison have achieved some leverage over the all-powerful imprisoners.

The hunger strike may, like the politics of street protest before it, lose its effectiveness. This could be a result of exhaustion on the part of its proponents, or a counter-initiative such as the planned "centralisation" of all hunger strikers in Bloemfontein. But the lessons of the early months of 1989 remain. Sooner or later, the extra-parliamentary movements will come up with something to replace the current tactics.

– Shaun Johnson, *Weekly Mail, 31.3.89*

See also: Jogging and jolling, Joking, Sanctuary

YELLOW

Yellow is the colour of resistance by conscientious objectors and anti-militarisation activists worldwide.

■ CO JAILED FOR 2 191 DAYS

DAVID Bruce's trial was rich in symbols. On Monday afternoon when he was sentenced, Bruce and his supporters wore yellow chrysanthemums and daisies – a sign, said ECC national secretary Alastair Teeling-Smith, of solidarity with war resisters which dated back to Vietnam. When a moist-eyed Bruce was led away from weeping friends by uniformed policemen, many supporters threw their yellow flowers on to the steps leading to the cells below the court.

– Weekly Mail, 29.7.88

■ ANTI-CONSCRIPTION PROTEST

CRIES of "Viva the ECC!" and "Down with the SADF!" rang out at the gates of Cape Town's Castle this week as a 400-strong march of conscientious objectors and their supporters reached its destination.

Abashed soldiers first hesitated, then accepted yellow chrysanthemums offered "in the name of peace" as the crowd, standing under a yellow banner proclaiming "Support Objectors: Stop the Call Up", cheered and applauded.

An old cannon had its mouth filled with flowers and a young national serviceman had the pockets and buttonholes of his uniform similarly decorated.

The marchers had come to deliver the names of the 771 conscientious objectors countrywide who recently declared their refusal to serve in the SADF, and to hand over demands that conscription be scrapped and that jailed COs be released.

Permission had earlier been granted for the march, which attracted crowds of bystanders as it snaked through the city.

As the marchers – six abreast and walking with arms linked – moved down Adderley Street, a middle-aged white man said to his companion: "You can see they're all poofters."

– Weekly Mail, 6.10.89

See also: Conscientious objection, Symbolic action

158

YES

Much of nonviolent action involves saying "No!" However, there are modes of NVA, often called conscientious affirmation, that involve saying "Yes!" – asserting values perceived to be just or right. Saying "Yes!" can involve civil disobedience but the emphasis falls on promoting what is right rather than attacking what is wrong. It respects the conscience of those behaving unjustly, and appeals to their capacity to recognise and follow the right and better path.

■ WHY I MARCHED – by GORDON OLIVER

MANY people have asked me why I as Mayor of Cape Town participated in Wednesday's march through the streets of Cape Town. Others have asked me: Was it a very difficult decision? Did it require much anguish on my part to come to that decision?

The background to my decision is quite simple. During the few months preceding my recent election to the office of mayor I made a point of visiting various members of the black and coloured communities, including those who had been detained by the police, in order to hear their views on how the mayor's office could be relevant to our city.

I approached them with no agenda and with the simple question: "What do you believe that I as mayor should be doing in our city?"

In every case the reply was: "Identify yourself openly with the issues that concern us directly in our daily lives."

Their response was given in total goodwill and appreciation of the fact that I, as incoming mayor, had made the effort to visit them and listen to their opinions.

On Thursday, the day before my installation as mayor, I heard the news that a number of people had died as a result of violence on the Cape Flats and that a memorial service was planned for Friday afternoon.

I felt that attending this service as mayor would give early effect to my decision to be amongst the people of the Cape Flats.

It was then that the Archbishop of Cape Town announced that a public march was to take place on Wednesday. I was asked by members of the press whether I would participate and I replied unhesitatingly that I intended to do so.

My decision was therefore not a difficult one to make because I had already decided that meaningful contact with, and support for, the people of the townships would be a top priority on the mayoral agenda.

Of course, the fact that it is illegal to march in the streets of the city was a factor, but I believed I should participate nevertheless.

By publicly standing my ground I have no doubt that I contributed in some small measure to the rethink at government level that led to the march being permitted. I say this with all humility but very mindful that civic leaders need to speak up more often. We need to use our influence in exerting positive pressure on the government towards bold political change.

– Sunday Star, 17.9.1989

■ "An example (of the power of saying 'Yes!') is the small group of American and SA Quakers and colleagues who decided in 1980 to travel together in a railway coach reserved for blacks only.

"Their intention was not primarily to commit civil disobedience, but to travel together and to share experiences with black South Africans. People in their coach talked freely with them.

"The Quakers told each conductor, and then several policemen, that they did not mean to cause trouble, but wanted to stay together. Eventually they were taken off the train to the nearest police station, cheered and encouraged by fellow passengers.

"After they had explained the spirit in which they had committed this illegal act the commandant said: 'Madam, you may ride together on the train, but next time please notify us,' and they were allowed to proceed on the next train.

"The story appeared in the newspapers and in an editorial denouncing petty apartheid."

– The Friend, 3.4.87

See also: Codes, Programmes, Satyagraha

BELOW
The march in Cape Town in September 1989 with the Mayor, Mr Gordon Oliver, in the lead.

Courtesy of THE ARGUS

ZABALAZA

"**B**lanket denunciations of violence by the churches place the counter-violence of the oppressed on the same level as the violence of the system that has driven the oppressed to such desperation. The Kairos Document pointedly asks: 'Would it be legitimate to describe both the physical force used by a rapist and the physical force used by a woman trying to resist the rapist as violence?' Are stones thrown by black youth (which as far as I know have not killed a single policeman) really commensurate with buckshot and real bullets fired by police (which in the last two years have killed around a thousand blacks including infants)?"

This is the question posed by American theologian and activist Walter Wink after a visit to SA in 1986. He was describing a background of equivocation against which the idea or theory of nonviolence has suffered a form of devaluation.

And yet the practice of nonviolent action in SA amounts to what he described even then, before the defiance victories of 1989, as "probably the largest grassroots eruption of diverse nonviolent strategies in a single struggle in human history".

Wink believed nonviolent structures should be put in place in SA, "capable of galvanising a lightning response by precommitted clergy who have already settled in advance the key questions about tactics, rationale and readiness to risk". Why not involve laity as well, he asked, and referred to a network of 80 000 people in the United States who had "pledged in advance that if significant military escalation by the US takes place in Central America, they will commit acts of civil disobedience or engage in nonviolent demonstrations. Training in nonviolence is a condition of this pledge."

Without asserting that the situation in SA and the Philippines under Ferdinand Marcos are similar, he suggested there are lessons to be learnt from the struggle that brought President Corazon Aquino to power there in February 1986.

The churches' leadership was involved in nonviolence training and a nonviolence movement was formed a year and a half before the crisis. Cory Aquino, whose husband Ninoy converted to Gandhian nonviolence after studying violent revolutions during his imprisonment, was herself involved in the movement's strategy sessions in the period after his assassination and before the crisis that was resolved with a nonviolent victory in one of the most remarkable chapters of world history.

■ THE UNARMED FORCES OF THE PHILIPPINES

THE overthrow of the Marcos regime in the Philippines was marked by its use of active nonviolence. Corazon Aquino, who was to take over from this tyrant, urged the use of nonviolence from the start of her campaign. The following events took place in Manila during the last four days before the Marcos regime was toppled.

A drama was unfolding at the other end of Manila, outside Camp Crame, where Defence Minister Enrile and General Ramos had defected from the 300 000-strong armed forces of the Philippines with a few hundred troops, declaring allegiance to Corazon Aquino.

Sister Milar Rocco was teaching her students about active nonviolence when she heard the news. Enrile and Ramos were expecting to be bombed at Camp Crame.

Although the situation was very frightening, the students were immediately ready to go to the camp.

When they got there they were confronted by soldiers still loyal to Marcos. The students offered the soldiers food and talked with them.

That evening fifty of the soldiers said they wanted to surrender. The nuns formed a big chain around them and slowly led the soldiers to Camp Crame, not knowing who was more afraid, they or the soldiers.

In the meantime calls went out over Radio Veritas, the Catholic station that provided reliable news in a country where the media were controlled by Marcos, for people to place their unarmed bodies between the defectors under Enrile and Ramos and the government troops.

The response of the people was amazing. From metropolitan Manila and the surrounding provinces people poured into the streets leading to Camp Crame.

They stayed day after day and through the nights, singing, praying and talking. A remarkable spirit prevailed. There were no pickpockets and no crimes. People shared food and water while others opened their homes to strangers for the use of toilets and a place to rest.

After thousands had gathered at Camp Crame, two airforce planes were sent to bomb the camp.

When the lead pilot saw the hundreds of thousands of people on two highways crisscrossing the camp's boundaries, it looked like a mammoth human cross. At that moment, he said, the hair on his head stood up and he felt it was a sign from God. Instead of dropping their bombs, both pilots flew to Clark Air Base and asked for asylum.

When armoured columns were sent in to clear out the highways and take over the camp, the people stood fast.

They surged towards the tanks and armoured personnel carriers, tied yellow ribbons on the gun barrels and offered the soldiers gifts of food, candy and garlands of flowers.

Sister Clare Joseph entreated the troops: "Pray with us. If you can't do it aloud, you can do it with your heart."

One eighty-year-old woman held a crucifix before a tank and said: "Stop! You can kill me but don't kill the young people here." The commander came down and embraced her.

A Marine colonel interviewed later said: "I was trained to deal with enemy soldiers and with rebels and I knew exactly how to handle them.

"But when my men and I approached the unarmed friendly people, I did not know what to do. There were pregnant women and little children there that reminded us of our own families.

"I knew that if I did not clear the road and follow my orders I would be shot. But I also knew that if I did that, I would have to violate my conscience."

– Crisis News, April 1988

From September 1984 to September 1989, SA was caught up in what became known as a "spiral of violence". Seen from the eye of the storm, it is not surprising that nonviolence was seldom identified by name as an effective means of struggle.

umZabalazo, the struggle, has been bitter, a long road marked by milestones bearing the names of martyrs like Steve Biko, who died in detention, and others who died in unexplained circumstances.

"Abduction, torture and death at the hands of clandestine forces are fast becoming a pattern of the war against opponents of apartheid," *New Nation* observed in February 1988.

And yet, despite the suffering, there has remained in SA a form of fellowship, of goodwill, that astounds observers. Theologian Gabriel Setiloane, of UCT's Department of Religious Studies, contends that "the recorder of history, being Western, has missed a very important point, namely that the African struggle is essentially a religiously inspired struggle".

The "reservoir of goodwill" South Africans like to speak of is actually, Setiloane suggests, the African understanding of community as the totality of everything that exists, seen and unseen.

The norm in that cosmic community is known in Setswana as "lotsididi", or "coolness", and this "placid harmony of the community of nature" is disrupted by injustice and avarice, among other things. Setiloane says that those responsible for injustice in SA have flouted this understanding of community and disturbed its "coolness", setting in motion an evil wish which afflicts not only the wrongdoers but the whole society.

The African remedy is a session of healing, a feast paid for by the wrongdoers and presided over by the ancestors, who are both the owners of the land and the guardians of morality. At this feast the wrongdoers would "confess the error of their ways and receive forgiveness and restoration and confirmation of their 'botho' or human-ness from the total community".

Setiloane asks: "Is not this feast and come-together of all the elements of the community, which African divination reveals to us, the national convention which has been the cry of the aggrieved of this land for so long?"

(Tlhagale and Mosala (eds): *Hammering Swords into Ploughshares – Essays in Honour of Archbishop Mpilo Desmond Tutu,* Skotaville, 1986)

In 1990, leading establishment politicians and theologians recanted and confessed, and discussions started on the preparation of the negotiating table – offering the hope that the violence which had gone senselessly spiralling on might stop. But the violence served as a reminder that conflict must be expected even in a normalised society, and that the need for nonviolent structures and intervention remained.

ABBREVIATIONS

Actstop	Action Committee to Stop Evictions
ANC	African National Congress
CIS	Centre for Intergroup Studies
Cosatu	Congress of South African Trade Unions
Cradora	Cradock Residents' Association
DET	Department of Education and Training
ECC	End Conscription Campaign
Fawu	Food and Allied Workers' Union
Idasa	Institute for a Democratic Alternative for South Africa
IFOR	International Fellowship of Reconciliation
JMC	Joint Management Centre
Jodac	Johannesburg Democratic Action Committee
MDM	Mass Democratic Movement
MDEM	Mass Democratic Education Movement
NECC	National Education Crisis Committee
NIC	Natal Indian Congress
NUM	National Union of Mineworkers
Numsa	National Union of Metal Workers of South Africa
Nusas	National Union of South African Students
NV	Nonviolent/Nonviolence
NVA	Nonviolent action
PAC	Pan Africanist Congress
PE	Port Elizabeth
PFP	Progressive Federal Party
PTSA	Parent-teacher-student association
PWV	Pretoria-Witwatersrand-Vereeniging (area)
SABC	South African Broadcasting Corporation
SACC	South African Council of Churches
SACOS	South African Council on Sport
SACP	South African Communist Party
SADF	South African Defence Force
SANSCO	South African National Students' Congress
SASPU	South African Students' Press Union
Sayco	South African Youth Congress
STYCO	Southern Transvaal Youth Congress
SUCA	Students' Union for Christian Action
TRAC	Transvaal Rural Action Committee
UCT	University of Cape Town
UDF	United Democratic Front
UNESCO	United Nations Education and Social Committee
UWC	University of the Western Cape
Wits	University of the Witwatersrand
WPCC	Western Province Council of Churches

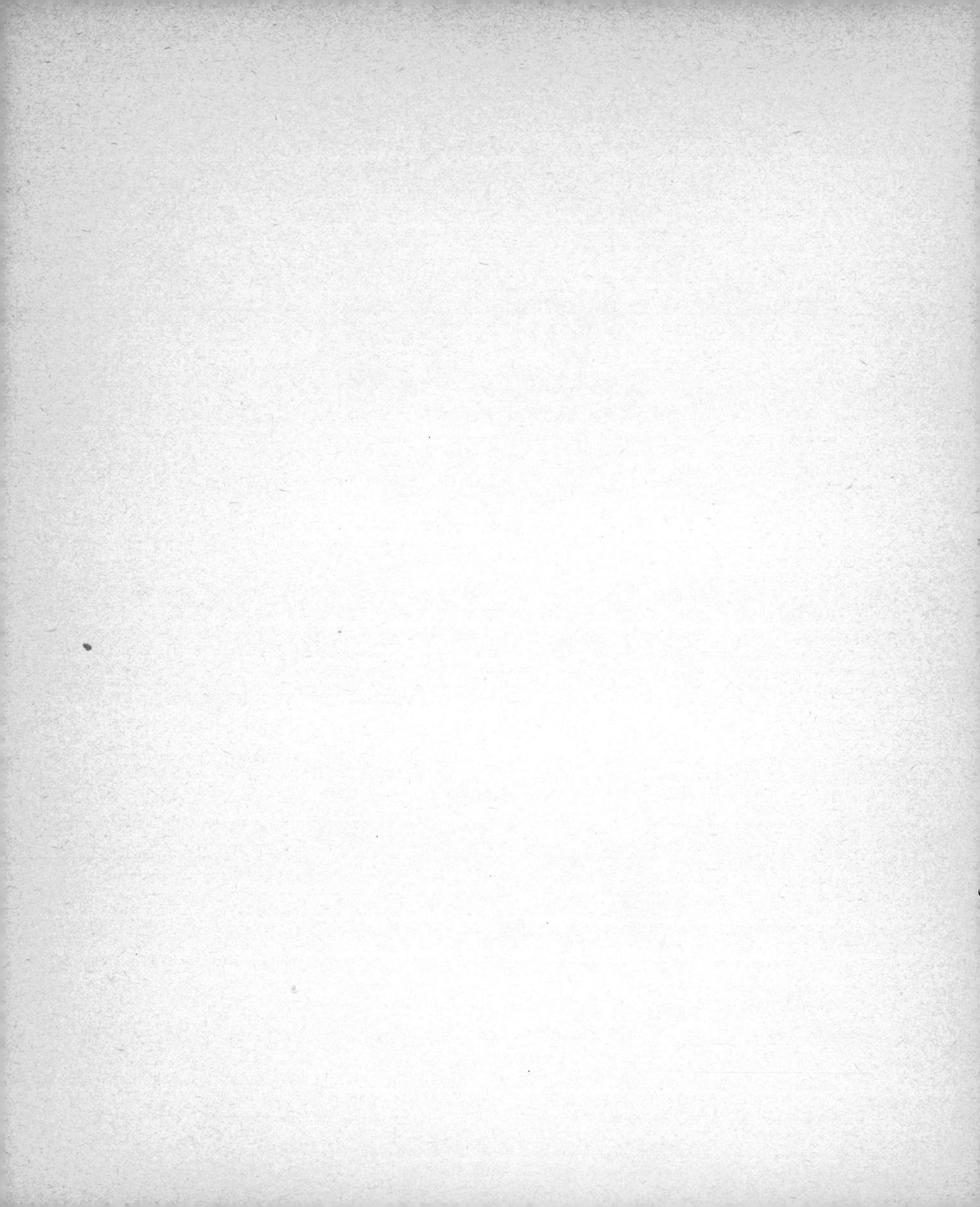